Where Have All the
Woolly Mammoths Gone?
A Small Business Survival Manual

Ted S. Frost

Parker Publishing Company, Inc.
West Nyack, New York

Library of Congress Cataloging in Publication Data

Frost, Ted S.
 Where have all the woolly mammoths gone?

 1. Small business--Management. 2. Small business.
I. Title.
HD69.S6F76   658'.022   75-28234
ISBN 0-13-957142-6

Printed in the United States of America

To all my clients, past and present, God Bless 'em, from whom, I'm afraid, I've learned far more than they ever learned from me.

Benefit from the
Experiences of Others

Too soon we get old;
too late we get smart.

Old German Proverb

This book is composed of gray hairs and ulcers. Mine, my clients' and my friends' . . . I am a C.P.A. My clients are all small businesses—shops, garages, small factories, stores, restaurants, contractors, sales reps— things like that. Over the years I have observed first-hand many hundreds of these small businesses. I have watched them being born, struggle, grovel, flourish, wither, boom, split, merge, and oftentimes go broke and die out, for small businesses these days have a rough row to hoe.

This is a book of practical advice for present and prospective small businessmen. It is intended to show the person in business for himself how to survive and, if he is lucky, how to succeed. The advice to be passed on has been distilled from the painful experiences of my many small business clients. It has also been taken in part from my own, for I, too, am a small businessman. Many of my suggestions are unorthodox. They are not the sort of things you would learn in a college business administration course. Nevertheless, they are realistic and practical. They are taken from my observations as a C.P.A. of thousands of real-life business experiences.

Experience is unquestionably the best teacher. Unfortunately, she is usually late to school. By the time experience teaches most of us our lessons in the school of hard knocks, the ship of opportunity has already passed us by.

Here, within these pages, I present you with a priceless opportunity—namely, the chance to learn ahead of time the things experience has taught others. Here is the chance to learn vicariously the hard-knock practical facts of business life without spending the time nor enduring the pain and agony that usually accompanies them.

One aspect of growing older seems to be the development of an overwhelming impulse to give out unsolicited advice. It is as though, after stumbling through a lifetime of blunders, we are biologically programmed to pass the lessons learned from our mistakes and experiences on to other generations. In today's fast-paced world, this sometimes seems a futile activity. Life situations for others are never exactly the same as our own. Besides, most people hate listening to advice to begin with. Nevertheless, it is human nature for those of us who have already been down the road to want to warn the others following. Our footprints may be erased by the winds of time and a changing environment, yet, we know that those following must still pass through similar terrain.

Even if our listeners take no action immediately on our words of wisdom, later on they may recognize their mistakes a little sooner. If I cause even this, I will consider my mission accomplished.

So here, for your benefit, are the things that I and many of my clients have belatedly learned over the years—the things that we wish we had known when we first started out in business. May you be able to profit from them.

Ted S. Frost, C.P.A.

Contents

1

The American Dream

America, thou has it better
Than our old continent . . . .
Within, naught restrains thee
From a livelier era;
No useless memories
Of unforgotten strife.
Face Thy future with happiness!

Goethe

For two hundred years, America has been known as the "land of the second chance." Like flocks of birds fleeing winter, millions of hairy-faced little peasant immigrants swarmed here over the years. A prime motive for leaving their homelands was that here in America they had the chance to get ahead.

Back in the "Old Country," they had belonged to hereditary peasant societies only one step removed from the feudal system of the Middle Ages. As peasants, our forefathers' status was ascribed rather than achieved. Moving to a virgin, expanding America gave most of them the first chance they had ever had to work their way up the social-economic ladder. As my Great-Grandmother from The Old Country used to say, "Life was hard homesteading among the buffalo and the Indians. Some of my children turned out good

9

and some turned out not so good, but at least here in America how they turned out depended upon them." This was the attraction—the chance to get ahead based upon your own merits—the chance to be master of your own destiny.

This attitude, this spirit of upward mobility, became part of our national folkways. In America, there was opportunity. Most took advantage of it by establishing their own enterprises. They no longer served as vassals, peasants, and servants. Instead, they became independent farmers, merchants, and craftsmen. Starting your own business became a way of life—the way to get ahead—the way to become free and independent. So it came to pass that in America a career in small business became a historical tradition. The American Dream became Adam Smith's economic model of many small, competing, free enterprises.

Comes now, the machine age, the industrial revolution, burgeoning technology and requirements of vast sums of capital. . . . Today, we are anything but a nation of small farmers and small businessmen. Today, America's economic power is concentrated in the hands of a relatively small number of large corporations. There are approximately 1,500,000 corporations in the United States. Of these, a mere 1% (15,000) control 80% of all corporate assets. A miniscule 0.05% (500) control 50% of all corporate assets. Private enterprise has become an upside down pyramid. The 500 largest industrial corporations have 10 times more assets and sales than the 500 second largest industrials.

As a result of this concentration, we are now mainly a nation of employees, working either for the government or for a small number of large businesses. Out of a total civilian work force of 60 million or so, approximately 20 million, or one-third, work for a comparative handfull of companies—one of 750! In terms of the total work force—civilian and government—22% work for the government. This means that over one-half of all employed persons in this country work either for the government or for one of only 750 companies!

Yet, tradition lingers on. Americans, in large numbers, still keep trying to become their own bosses. New small businesses are constantly being formed all over America. The turnover, however, is rapid. While 400,000 new businesses a year are started, nearly that same number go out of business each year. Many others change hands. Dun & Bradstreet estimates that only one out of every three businesses is still in existence four years after being started.

Despite the concentration of economic power and despite small business' high mortality rate, going into business for oneself is still a way of life in this country. Most people dream and scheme of it at one time or another in their lives. However, out there in the shadows the voracious small business mortality rate lurks, waiting to gobble them up.

Obviously there are problems in owning your own business. What are the problems and what causes them? Why are so many small businesses squeezed out of existence and why don't all the myriad of those that do exist, own a bigger piece of the economic pie?

2

The Problems

The chance of a newcomer becoming an established member of the business community is sadly slight. He carries on until his funds are exhausted and then disappears from the scene. His place is taken by another hopeful, certain that he has the abilities which will permit him to succeed where his predecessor failed. . . . Unaware of the odds against them, and largely ignorant of the weapons of trade, prospective proprietors march stolidly to the ambush.

Temporary National
Economic Committee

The woolly mammoth was a fabulous creature. It was huge and shaggy with enormous curved tusks. Thousands of years ago it galumphed around the Northern Hemisphere undoubtedly making a lot of noise and not much caring about what got in its way. The woolly mammoth was rugged and independent and seemingly destined to survive against the forces of nature a long, long time. All of a sudden, about 9,000 years ago, it became extinct. The reason why has always been a mystery to those scientists who contemplate such things. The last few years, however, some scientists finally think they have figured it out. Their theory is that the woolly mammoth became extinct because our paleolithic hunting ancestors killed them all.

How ironic! That a creature so big and rugged and independent should be wiped out by a bunch of puny, grubby, smelly little cavemen. But they were organized cavemen and they possessed technology. They worked together and produced fire and spears. They lit torches and made noise and drove the woolly mammoths over cliffs and into bogs and traps. They divided and conquered. They separated the immature and weak mammoths from the strong and then surrounded and butchered them. After awhile, guess what? No more woolly mammoths!

There is an analogy here, for today other organized little men also possessing great technology are threatening another rugged creature—the small independent businessman. Just like the woolly mammoth, the small businessman of today is in grave danger of becoming extinct. Hordes of men banded together into huge corporate structures are, with their organizational efficiencies and economic clout, making it impossible for small businessmen to coexist.

The evidence is all around us. The small farm has become a corporate operation with headquarters in town. The mamma-papa grocery store has been replaced by the chain supermarkets. The independent "filling station" of Gasoline Alley has become a stylized Standard or Shell station. The small restaurant in the middle of the block has given way to Howard Johnson's or Colonel Sander's Kentucky Fried Chicken. The family doctor has turned into a large impersonal clinic of specialists. The local department store has become a member of a national chain. The local factory—a subsidiary, etc., etc.

Consolidate-incorporate; multiply-stratify; reorganize-specialize; departmentalize-depersonalize. We are fast becoming a nation of bureaucratic superorganisms. The trend is obvious and it is becoming a crescendo.

Governmental statistics confirm the fact that small business is a shrinking factor in this nation's economy. Over the last century, the number of farms and businesses have steadily declined in relation to the number of workers. In 1880, there were 359.7 farm and business enterprises per thousand workers. In 1970, there were only 137.7.

Year	Number of Farms and Businesses (In Thousands)	Number of Workers* (In Thousands)	Number of Farms and Businesses Per Thousand Workers
1880	5,461	15,181	359.7
1890	7,023	21,524	326.3
1900	7,903	29,070	271.9
1910	8,814	37,370	235.8
1920	8,960	42,430	211.2
1930	9,113	48,830	186.6
1940	9,590	52,150	183.9
1950	9,997	63,858	156.6
1960	11,172	72,142	154.9
1970	12,001	85,903	137.7

*For the years 1880-1930, the figures represent gainfully occupied persons 10 years old and over; for the year 1940, gainfully occupied persons 14 years old and over; for the years 1950-1970, persons in the labor force 16 years old and older.

Sources: *Statistical Abstract of the United States; The First Two Years: Problems of Small Firm Growth and Survival* by Kurt Mayer and Sidney Goldstein, published by the Small Business Administration.

While small businesses have been declining, big businesses have been increasing on a per capita basis. The bigger the business, the bigger the rate of increase.

In recent times, corporations with assets of $100,000 to $1 million have been increasing at a rate of 3% per capita per year; corporations with assets of $1 million to $10 million have been increasing at a rate of 4% per capita per year; corporations with assets of $10 million to $100 million have been increasing by 5% per capita per year; and corporations with assets of over $100 million have been increasing by 7% per capita per year. Clearly there is a persistent trend in this country towards bigger and bigger business entities.

The statistics as to gross sales volume are also alarming. The percentage of the nation's total annual sales has been decreasing for each of the foregoing business size categories except one—the very largest corporations, those with assets exceeding $100 million. Over the last ten years, this small coterie of giants has sucked another 11.1% of total sales into its collective maw, going from 27.6% of the nation's total sales to 38.7%.

If you extrapolate these trends, the results are alarming. If present trends continue, by 1984 my children will be dealing with 34% fewer business entities, on a per capita basis, than when I first started out in business. By 1984, two-tenths of one percent of all U.S. corporations will account for over 90% of all business sales. By then we will have indeed become prisoners of an all encompassing oligarchy.

Besides declining in numbers, small businesses have another problem that the foregoing statistics do not reflect—namely, instability. There is a great deal of turnover among individual small business units. Not only is the number of small businesses per capita declining, but the composition of their individual indentities changes rapidly.

A study by the U.S. Department of Commerce* for the years 1947 through 1954 indicated that chances were 50% that a new small business would not last two years, 66-2/3% that it would not last 4 years, and 80% that it would not live to the age of ten. Another study for the years 1955 through 1958 by two Brown University professors pointed out that of 4.3 million firms in operation January 1, 1955, only one third were still doing business under the same management four years later. The authors commented:

> Underlying the slow growth and small net changes of aggregate numbers is a persistent succession of business entities and discontinuances and a hard struggle for individual survival. . . . Some variation of experience does occur in different communities, in different fields of business, and under changing business conditions, but high mortality is not primarily a cyclical phenomenon. On the contrary, it is all-pervasive; the most striking fact is the regularity of failure and the persistence of high turnover rates.**

*"Age and Life Expectancy of Business Firms," *Survey of Current Business,* Dec. 1955, U.S. Department of Commerce.

***The First Two Years: Problems of Small Firm Growth and Survival,* by Kurt B. Mayer and Sidney Goldstein, Brown University, page 5.

All of these statistics and studies merely confirm what empirical observations tell us. Inspect your personal environment these days and you will find very few items in it that are capable of being produced by small business: color TV, polyester fabrics, never-wax vinyl floors, rotary engine automobiles, direct dial telephones, microwave ovens, wonder drugs, formica table tops, polypropylene chairs, food preservatives, nuclear power plant electricity, mechanized food harvesting equipment, eyeglasses that darken in the sunlight, artificial food sweeteners, enzyme detergents—we are surrounded by miracle materials and magic products. We live encased in technological cocoons that only the most complicated of industrial complexes can produce and maintain. Commercial enterprises these days require complicated technology, specialized processes, and enormous gobs of capital. As a result, opportunities for small business shrink every year.

Stop and think about it, little small businessman. What with today's fantastic communications, incredible technology, and tremendous rate of change, how can you possibly compete with Big Business?

How can you set up an efficient production line when you have small production runs?

How can you compete with national advertising and standardized products?

How can you attract a cynical, mobile customer who doesn't even know that you exist?

How can you compete with Big Business' specialized experts when you, all by yourself, must have expertise in hundreds of different subjects?

How can you create new products when such large amounts of capital are required for development?

How can you, a small firm, possibly compete with Big Business' outside sources of capital, political clout, prestige, computerized efficiency, departmentalized specialization, vertical and horizontal monopolies?

The awful truth is—you can't!! Let's face it. Small business' biggest enemy these days is Big Business. Big Business' domination creeps further and further into every nook and cranny of the economy. Small business is being continually forced onto higher ground—where the soil is barren and the vegetation sparse.

Small business, in other words, is having to take to the hills. The idea of starting a small business these days and having it grow into a large enterprise with your name as founder is fast becoming a myth—an anachronistic saga. As John Kenneth Galbraith says, " . . . it is now recognized that this is not the age of the small man."

It is increasingly apparent that the role of individual effort in our society is becoming obsolete. Even the powers-that-be are coming around to recognizing the problem:

The U.S. Secretary of Commerce:

> How can we protect and encourage the shopkeeper so his business can become a chain, or at least live on as a neighborhood fixture?

Senator William Proxmire:

> While the Congress and administration battle to save jobs and business for Penn Central, Lockheed, Boeing, and the automobile Big Three, companies that admittedly have great impact on the economy, smaller firms are finding it ever more difficult to keep their heads above red ink. And these smaller firms simply don't have the visibility or the raw political power to get the type of federal attention lavished on their big brothers.

The U.S. Attorney General:

> The danger that this super concentration poses to our economic, political, and social structure cannot be overestimated. Concentration of this magnitude is likely to eliminate existing and future competition. . . . It creates structures whose enormous physical and psychological resources pose substantial barriers to smaller firms wishing to participate in a competitive market.

Today, Big Business is small business' mortal enemy and it is no contest. Yet, paradoxically, most small businessmen can't seem to get this through their heads. To most small businessmen, business is business and they relate and identify with any form of business whether it be General Motors or the corner hot-dog stand. So they go on renewing their subscriptions to *Business Week* and spouting the same old cliches at Rotary meetings . . . about the superiority of our free enterprise system; the desirability of laissez faire; and the evils of governmental control. It is pathetic, really, listening to the typical small businessman identify with Big Business—as though he belonged to the same club.

The facts are:

1. The free enterprise system in this country, in the traditional sense, hardly exists.

2. If laissez faire were the order of the day, most small businesses would already be extinct.

3. If it weren't for governmental restrictions and controls, we would all by now be working for a handful of monopolies.

The facts are that there are actually two quite different species of business—Big Business and small business. Small businesses are like small towns. They are tribal affairs where everyone knows everyone else and where a high degree of informality and overlap exists. Seat-of-the-pants operation is the rule. Big Businesses, on the other hand, are like large cities. They are impersonal, compartmentalized, and stratified.

So what if Big Business is large and impersonal? At the same time, Big Business is also very efficient and extremely productive. Is that bad? Look at all that we have as a result of it. Look at the huge quantities of goodies that giant corporations belch forth for our pleasure, comfort, amusement, and consumption. From a materialistic point of view, never before has so large a proportion of any population ever had it so good.

Yet, as our hippie-culture youth seem to have discovered, something is missing. Big Business' environment is a spiritual bore!

How much sense of worth, how much stimulation, how much dignity is there to be found in tightening seven bolts on a production line?

Or existing as a clerk shuffling papers at a desk surrounded by hundreds of other drones?

Or serving an endless array of faces whom you have never seen before and will never see again?

Working for a giant corporate bureaucracy as an anonymous supernumerary, one out of a cast of thousands?

Being processed by number, rather than by name?

How many Big Business employees are happy? Challenged? Stimulated?

Except for those at the top, damn few. Ironically, these are satisfactions that only small business seems to be able to provide.

Here is the excuse for trying to save small business from extinction. Here is the rationale for farm subsidies and the Small Business Administration.

For the worth of small business lies outside of its contribution to our economy. Its economic contribution is puny, being mainly that of consumption. The worth of small business is of a higher calling. Small business engages men's spirits. It provides outlets for our biologically rooted psychic needs. Small business has *soul.*

Unfortunately, spiritual worth does not guarantee survival—as many a martyr will testify. So the question remains—how do we, the nation's small businesses survive? Our survival depends upon quick wits, aggressiveness, knowledge, daring, flexibility, and plenty of objective thinking. These qualities and aptitudes will be stressed in more detail later on. The complete strategy for survival will be developed in chapters to follow. For the time being, however, we can say that the first rule is, simply, stay out of Big Business' way. Do not try to compete with the products Big Business already produces and do not try to compete where Big Business already exists. Go to those suburbs and small towns where Big Business is not yet established. Keep your products and services simple. Complexity in either product or service requires large amounts of time and capital—neither one of which you, the small businessman, can provide. Innovate, probe, seek. You must go out and find yourself a niche in territories that Big Business has not yet usurped—and hope that life there does not become too crowded.

As a C.P.A., I constantly have people entering my office seeking advice on how to go into business for themselves. In most instances, these individuals are emotionally involved with the *idea* of being their own boss. No one to tell them what to do, no one to order them around, no one to take advantage of them, no one to profit from the fruits of their labor, no more dull tasks to perform, no more time clocks to punch. They become so in love with these thoughts that many tend to pursue half-baked plans as to what they are going to do and how they are going to do it. They grasp the first opportunity that comes along regardless of how inappropriate it is to them personally.

Before assuming the risks involved in starting your own business, you should by all means, analyze your goals, your motives, and your emotional makeup. Flight from boredom should not be the only motive for going into business for yourself. A small business career will cure your sense of boredom all right, but unless you are emotionally suited to withstand the hassles and problems of small business life, you may find you have merely traded your present form of unhappiness for another variety. You may find that you have sacrificed the security and seniority of a nice stable job for a life of worry, frustration, long hours and low pay; and, if your business fails and you have to return to your previous occupation, you may find you have lost your place in line.

On the other hand, if you are a certain kind of person, going into business for yourself will very probably be the smartest move you have ever made. Being your own boss may give you a sense of fulfillment and excitement that you have never before experienced. The freedoms and challenges of small business life may more than compensate for the greater remuneration you may have had had you stayed an employee and worked your way up the corporate pyramid. But it all depends upon the type of person you are.

This book may, in some places, sound like a layman's version of *Psychology Today*. This is because personality traits are so very important in determining whether or not a small businessman is successful. The pressures, complexities, and uncertainties found in the business world today require as never before the ability to act rationally in a consistent manner. At the same time, a small businessman must be able to harness the power of his emotional drives. The secret to success depends, in other words, more upon the internal composition of a businessman's own mind than it does upon the possession of external abstract knowledge. It takes a special kind of person to become a success in small business these days. And what sort of person might that be?

3

Are You an Alpha?

He was a yelling, wiry, malevolent, sneevily, snively
Bully who had quelled all insurgents for miles around.
I did not know one kid who was not afraid of Dill,
mainly because Dill was truly aggressive. This kind of
aggression later in life is often called "Talent" or
"Drive". . . .*

Jean Shepherd,
In God We Trust, All Others Pay Cash

What is the single most important quality necessary for
success in small business?

You may be surprised to learn that intelligence is not the
answer. Now, of course, a high degree of intelligence is certainly
useful in small business as it is in nearly every other field of
endeavor. However, intelligence is not a prerequisite. Neither is
personality, perseverance, high evergy level, resourcefulness, or
sound judgment.

All of these characteristics are mighty useful to have but
there is one characteristic that, above all others, is absolutely
essential. Aggression! If you are ever going to make a go of things,
you've got to be aggressive! Small businessmen run the complete

---

*Quoted from Jean Shepherd, *In God We Trust, All Others Pay Cash.*
© Doubleday and Company.

spectrum as far as personality traits and mental capacities go, but the successful ones I have known have all had one common characteristic—they have been as aggressive as hell! I don't mean physical pugnaciousness. The aggression I refer to is the strong, general, overall desire to dominate—the urge to compete and prevail—the drive of one who wants to impose his will upon others.

Those small businessmen lacking a high degree of this characteristic just don't, as a rule, do well. A scientific description of what I am talking about lies in the biological concept of the so-called "Alpha."

Biologists have long observed that there exists within the population of most animal species certain dominant individuals known as Alphas. Alphas are characterized by their aggressive, domineering behavior. Alphas are the ones who wind up having the best food, the choicest mates, and the most desirable territories. Whatever the popular status symbol may be, Alphas are the ones who corner the market.

Next, come a group of individuals known as Betas. Betas strive to dominate and compete also, but unfortunately (for them), they just don't have what it takes. Consequently, Betas wind up being dominated by Alphas.

Finally, there are the Omegas. Omegas are life's perpetual losers—the Charlie Browns of the species. Omegas are the ones who have lost so often they have dropped out. They don't even bother trying to compete anymore.

These categories have been observed in practically every animal species—from fish to rats to monkeys to man. Nobody seems to know yet what it is exactly that causes a successful Alpha. Important ingredients making up Alphaness seem to be virility, courage, energy, strength, confidence, ambition, and luck. Whatever it is that creates an Alpha, one thing is for sure—they make awfully good businessmen!

Most of the successful businessmen I know are pretty tough characters. They are gutsy, aggressive, self-assured and competitive. Definitely Alphas. The stress and strain of striving and competing doesn't bother them. As a matter of fact, they seem to enjoy and thrive on it. Alphas have been shown to be much less prone to heart attacks and ulcers than Betas.

So, if you think you are an Alpha, going into business for yourself is probably a good idea. Owning your own business may give you the chance to be the despot that by nature you are.

On the other hand, if you are a Beta or an Omega, take my advice and forget it. If you are a Beta or an Omega and you go into business for yourself, you will probably wind up being both unsuccessful and miserable and you will increase your chances of having a heart attack or ulcers about four times over besides.

4

Machiavellian Man

"People Are No Damn Good"
by William Steig
(Used with permission of Thomas Y. Crowell Company, Inc.)

It is interesting how some people are so adept at manipulating and taking advantage of others. Some businessmen have the absolutely uncanny ability of being able to climb right over the heads of practically everyone they come into contact with. These types fascinate me. Observing one of them in action stimulates my sense of morbid curiosity—like watching a snake hypnotize a rat.

Psychologists recently have become interested in the nature of people who possess this trait. They call such individuals "Machiavellians" in honor of Niccolo di Bernado Machiavelli, the fifteenth century analyst of politicians and their practices.

Machiavellian people, according to psychologists, have four basic characteristics:

1. They are not concerned with morality in the conventional sense. That is, they see nothing wrong with taking advantage of people. Their philosophy seems to be that people are basically fools, so why not take advantage of them?

2. They are cool and detached with other people. They do not become emotionally involved. They view other people as foreign objects rather than as being members of the same tribe.

3. They actually enjoy conning others. They derive satisfaction from the game rather than the goals—the means rather than the end. Like cats, they enjoy toying with mice.

4. Surprisingly, they are not psychotic. On the contrary, they have an undistorted view of reality. They deal with others in a cool, rational, realistic way.

A Machiavellian manipulator is basically insensitive to others. His insensitivity enables him to guiltlessly climb over others in order to achieve his own rational goals. Not being worn out emotionally by guilt feelings, he can be exceedingly persistent. The process of haggling and hassling doesn't exhaust him. Machiavellians can bargain all day long, if necessary, until their victims just plain give out.

The interesting thing, though, is this: According to psychologists, Machiavellianism usually develops at an early age. However, it isn't something that children are taught—rather, it seems to develop naturally as the result of children having victims to practice on. High Mach parents do not necessarily produce High Mach children. Instead, the converse is more often true. Children of Low Mach parents are more successful at manipulating their parents than those children with High Mach parents. They, therefore, learn Machiavellian skills at an early age. This means that many people are probably latent Machiavellians but, having been suppressed by their parents, they never had the chance to fully develop.

The implication is that if you are now a Low Mach, it is quite possible that you have within yourself the potential to become more of a manipulator. If you can learn to develop heretofore dormant Machiavellian skills you should by all means do so. Machiavellianism, along with Alphaness, will enhance your business proficiency greatly.

Of course, suggesting the development of Machiavellian attitudes in connection with successful small business management shocks and repulses people of intellectual bent. But, then, humanistic intellectuals all suffer the same misconception. They persist in assuming that every man deep down inside possesses the same noble, humane instincts they feel. They think that the only reason such instincts don't surface is because people have been corrupted by their environment. Thanks to Freud, they think that it is man's habitat rather than his inherited characteristics that causes him to be self centered. From the misty heights of their ivory towers, radical-chic double domes cannot perceive that all those masses swarming over the ground below them are Yahoos.

The moral is that if you are going to enter the business world, be prepared to leave your conventional morals behind.

If you have the need to be good, kind, vulnerable and accommodating to others, you had best provide outlets for such feelings in your personal life. The practice of these sentiments in the business world will inevitably cause you to be taken advantage of.

When I review in my mind the individual business failures I have known over the years, I am struck by the high proportion that have occurred to what you would call, Nice Guys. The S.O.B.'s on the other hand, always seem to survive.

The picture I paint so far of the archetypical successful businessman is not a pretty one.

The successful businessman often displays traits not in keeping with Christian-Judaic ethics. He, at times, is mean, petty, avaricious, selfish, devious and occasionally a liar. He is dedicated towards looking after his own narrow-minded self-interests. He does this with tenacious single-mindedness of purpose. He often hides behind hypocritical self-delusions. He looks at his business from the point of view that what is good for him is also good for the community.

The free enterprise system, in short, is a self-righteous con game. Swarms of businessmen are out there trying to obtain other people's dollars for as little in return as possible. The Satanic genius of the system is that it works! What could be a meaner motive than to use others in order to obtain a profit for ourselves? Instead of working for the common good of the tribe and for the welfare of our neighbors and comrades, we look out for ourselves.

Ironically, while groveling and clawing for profit, we are drawn into producing labor that is useful to the community as a whole. Like proverbial donkeys chasing proverbial carrots, we draw full loads behind us. The realization that this is so drives Communists crazy.

A successful businessman may not be nature's noblest handiwork, but, nevertheless, that is the way he is. If you are going to succeed, you had best conform. Let the meek inherit the earth. Meanwhile, the wheels of commerce must turn.

5

The Charlie Brown Syndrome

A man . . . with powers that have uniformly brought him success with place and wealth and friends and fame, is not likely to be visited by the morbid differences and doubts about himself which he had when he was a boy, whereas he who has made one blunder after another and still lies in the middle life among the failures at the foot of the hill is liable to grow all sicklied o'er with self-distrust, and to shrink from trials with which his powers can really cope.

William James

Some years ago a plastic surgeon named Maxwell Maltz wrote a popular self-help book titled, *Psycho-Cybernetics.* The book's theme is basically a power-of-positive thinking pump-yourself-up philosophy in the same genre as Norman Vincent Peale, Dale Carnegie, and others. Books of this ilk usually turn me off as I believe them to be largely ineffectual. Quick solutions to human personality problems have the bad habit of wearing off just as quickly as the solution's application.

Psycho-Cybernetics, however, is built around an intriguing idea. Maltz expounds on the psychological concept that people early in life develop a self-image of themselves. He explains that once our minds form this self-image, from that point on, regardless of its validity, we act as though it were true. Maltz believes that our actions, feelings, and behavior remain consistent with our self-image and that this starts a vicious circle of self-fulfilling behavior.

For example, suppose as a youngster you believed deep down inside that you were a poor student. According to Maltz, your subsequent behavior would then be consistent with this self-image in ways that would cause you to actually perform badly in school. You would neglect your homework or quickly lose interest in class, figuring "What's the use?" Your poor performance in school would then reinforce your original poor image of yourself, whereupon you would be all set up, cocked and loaded, ready for another round of poor performance.

What led Maltz to this conclusion was his experience as a plastic surgeon. Maltz often observed that, after converting an ugly face into a beautiful face, the attached person kept right on acting as though he or she were still ugly. Presumably even though the person's face had been beautified, his self-image remained ugly. The key to success, according to Maltz, is to change one's self-image. Psycho-Cybernetics describes how to go about changing your self-image when you feel yourself to be unworthy, inferior, undeserving, incapable, or in any other way, icky.

I think Maltz has something here. It has long been recognized that the opinion a person has of himself greatly influences his behavior. Self-esteem, or conversely, self-disesteem, is an important ingredient in a person's overall effectiveness.

Self-esteem or self-image is a beautiful explanation of why some people are failure-prone and seemingly can't stand success. Extreme examples of this mechanism are people who are chronically accident-prone, or the people police call, "victims walking around looking for murderers."

Every once in awhile, I come across a businessman who repeatedly comes right up to the brink of success or even crosses the threshold. Then for some stupid reason, this same individual, after having worked so hard and operated so competently up to this point, proceeds to go out and mess it all up. The unusual thing about this particular type of person is that, for him it is a constantly recurring pattern. There is the failure-prone salesman, for example, who works like mad putting together a big sale in his business—then, just when he has it, for some reason or other, he proceeds to bungle up the order and lose the business. Or there is the businessman who works diligently building up a sound, profitable business and then, once he has it, throws it away by goofing off, drinking, gambling, chasing women—whatever activities he can think of that will cause him to neglect his business.

Occasionally I am called upon to hire accounting personnel for clients. Some applicants that I interview seem to be exceptionally well qualified. Education, experience, appearance—everything about them looks good except for one peculiar fact. They have had numerous previous jobs or have been in numerous previous business ventures—all of which have come to grief. They have a million unfortunate stories of past woes. Nothing has ever seemed to work out for them. Invariably, whenever I have hired this type of individual, the same thing happens. They strike out in their new job also.

Do people like this feel themselves unworthy? Deficient? Unlovable? Do they, every once in awhile, have to go out and prove to themselves that their self-images are correct, that they are natural born losers? Is this why the comic strip hero, Charlie Brown, creates such universal empathy?

Psychological studies have been made of the factors contributing towards the development of high self-esteem. A person's early family life seems to be the biggest factor. These studies indicate that high self-esteem people tend to have had benevolent despots as parents. Parents who were able to communicate to the child that he was a significant person worthy of their abiding interest. Parents who were strict and consistent in the enforcement of rules but not harsh—being open to dissent and persuasion from the child.

I am not qualified to tell you how to go about changing your self-image. All I know is that I do encounter people in business who seem to experience recurring failures for no good reason at all. If your background has such a pattern to it, I suggest it might be a good idea to seek professional help before trying again. The small business world eats losers for breakfast.

6

Mind Over Matter

Motivation. A general term referring to factors within an organism that arouse and maintain behavior directed towards satisfying some need or drive or toward accomplishing a goal.

Development Psychology Today

I could not go very much further discussing what it is that helps cause small business success without saying something about motivation.

Motivation isn't important, it is everything. One of the coaches on my college rowing team, years ago, was a venerable old Englishman named George Pocock. George was a colorful philosopher out of whom wisdom oozed at every pore. Before a race, George used to say, "Boys, yu've gaught ti waunt't ti do it!" My teammates and I never quite realized what old George was getting at, at the time, which may have something to do with why we never won many crew races. However, as time goes by, George's words sink in deeper with every passing year. In order to accomplish anything, in order to achieve anything, you have to *want* to do it. You have to emotionalize your goals.

If you happen to be a member of the gifted one-in-a-million club, things fall into place without special effort. Otherwise, as a rule of life, whether it be sports or business, your chances of achievement vary in direct proportion to your desires. This is so regardless of the mental, emotional and physical baggage you carry. If you go to bed at night dreaming of your goal, if you constantly think about it during the day, if you want it so badly you can taste it and feel it—then sooner or later whatever potentialities you possess will be directed towards that end. When all of your brain waves are tuned in on the goal, then you have maximized your chances of success.

"Willing" your way to success may sound spooky but, to a certain extent, it works. Strong motivation overcomes an awful lot. Nearly all of us encounter from time to time people who have triumphed over great handicaps and personal disadvantages to achieve personal success.

I cannot overemphasize—the best chance of success lies in achieving the mental state of being willing to barter your very soul for the goal.

7

The Power of Intuitive Thinking

Most people who think they are thinking, are actually only rearranging their prejudices.

Knute Rockne

Intuitive wisdom is usually considered to be in the same category as home remedies for curing warts. Intuition has been looked down upon ever since the scientific method became established as the logical way to go about trying to understand the world.

It shouldn't be this way, really. There is more to intuition than blind hunch. Our minds are constantly picking up subliminal bits of information around us. Most experienced people use this stuff as a subconscious input into their decision making process. In addition, there is the matter of psychic phenomenon. More and more people are coming around to the viewpoint that ESP is for real. Many successful businessmen have vague feelings from time to time, about particular matters before them that influence their decisions greatly. As a friend of mine sometimes says, "It doesn't pass the smell test."

Most people feel this way on occasion. If they are educated, these feelings are apt to bother them. They usually brush them aside, because they think that giving in to them is akin to being superstitious. For example, how many times have you said to yourself after something turned out contrary to your outward expectations—"I knew I should/shouldn't have done that. I had a hunch it was the right/wrong thing to do." Yet, most people continue to suppress such feelings when they occur because at the time they cannot perceive any rational reason why they should feel the way they do.

When I was younger, I used to react this way myself. The many science courses I sat through during my schooling conditioned me to respect the logic of rational analysis. As a result, inductive and deductive reasoning became my bag. After graduating from college, I was convinced I could easily cut a swath through the crude business world. All I needed in order to achieve instant success was to apply the scientific method to business problems.

It has been a good many years now since I first tried using that approach. Many's the time since that I have lain awake at night trying to figure out why I fell flat on my face the preceding day. My conclusion is that logic is the substance that the road to hell is paved with.

Logical reasoning, after all, is no big deal. Most people are capable of it on occasion—if you give them an underlying *premise* to start with. That, however, is the problem. All logical arguments must start somewhere from a foundation of fundamental premises or presuppositions. If these are false, then, naturally, the whole train of logic that follows becomes mush.

Those businessmen who analyze every situation logically usually suffer from an occupational hazard. They tend to become overconfident of the rationality of their reasoning. The beauty of their logic blinds them. All too often their reasoned analysis covers a faulty premise lurking beneath the surface. Just when they think they have a situation all figured out and after they have committed themselves to it—zot! Out jumps the faulty premise.

The most common, I suppose, is the historical premise that what has happened in the past will continue happening in the future. I remember one small machine shop client, for example, who enjoyed a nice steady growth. Based on the pattern of his past business, he decided to acquire an enormously expensive computer-controlled milling machine. He was troubled by this decision and had to overcome grave feelings of anxiety and doubt before he bought it. His logic said *yes* but his intuition said *no*. Nevertheless, he went ahead and ordered the machine, figuring that it would give him a nice advantage over his competitors and that projected future earnings growth would make the payments. Unfortunately, this was a mistaken assumption, because 80% of his business was with one large aerospace company. Overcapacity among the airlines caused the aerospace company to suddenly suffer a severe decline. His orders dribbled down to a trickle. My client wound up in left field with a big, fat, expensive, unpaid for white elephant. The burden of carrying the milling machine's payments eventually caused him to go under.

The point is that it is worthwhile to pay attention to your intuitive sense about things. Wisdom is not always capable of being articulated into words. Our minds are constantly churning at a subverbal level. If you have vague, uneasy feelings about certain matters, do not be in a hurry to brush them aside. Try to figure out why you feel that way. What is it that brings out such feelings? They may be emotional, irrational reactions. They may be expressions of psychological hang-ups. On the other hand, they may be the result of your sixth-sense radar picking up vibrations that aren't readily apparent on the surface.

When you have a tough decision to make, do not be in such a hurry to go forward with a logical progression of thought. Instead, go backwards! Search out and examine your underlying premises—the things you may have subconsciously assumed when you started out. Most of our errors come from assumptions we are not even aware we have made. There was a saying among John F. Kennedy's advisors that the kind of people you have to be particularly wary of are those who possess the ability of being able to make a bad idea sound good. Too often this is exactly what we do to ourselves.

So, treat your intuitive instincts with respect. There is probably more common sense behind them than you realize.

8

Perspective and Goals

"Ascending and Descending" by Maurits Escher from the collection of C.V.S. Roosevelt, Washington, D.C.

If there is one single quality, the lack of which causes ruination in business more often than any other, it is perspective. Without a good sense of perspective, business management becomes a process of alternately overreacting and underreacting. Lack of perspective causes people to respond to stimuli rather than to causes. It makes them jump at loud noises, yet allows them to race speeding freight trains to the crossing.

It causes tunnel vision and can't-see-the-forest-for-the-trees, both common afflictions in the business world. Professor C. Northcote Parkinson describes lack of perspective in his "Law of the Point of Vanishing Interest." Parkinson notes that corporation directors will argue endlessly over such things as spending $5,000 on a new storage shed while simultaneously passing without comment appropriations costing millions of dollars. $5,000 they can relate to, but millions of dollars are beyond anyone's comprehension.

On a lesser scale, a small businessman will argue like mad over a 25 dollar increase in monthly rent for his business yet won't spend any time at all analyzing the suitability of its location, a factor that can mean thousands of dollars to him.

I continually encounter businessmen who act this way. They become intrigued with some small aspect of their business, which they proceed to beat to death, while they neglect more important affairs until their businesses begin to fall down around their ears.

They will do such things as:

Spend a lot of time harrassing a couple of $400 a month girls in the front office while ignoring the production people out in the plant who are costing $14,000 a month and who are featherbedding like mad.

Or, spend their time fussing around out in the plant doing a foreman's job when they should be out trying to generate more sales and new customers.

Or, knock themselves out trying to satisfy the whims of a few, small, vocal, marginal customers while neglecting the ones who are large and important but silent.

Or, be extremely cost conscious as to small office overhead items but be loose and lax as to granting credit and collecting delinquent accounts.

Many people carry on this way because they fear making

major decisions. By immersing themselves in a quagmire of small, petty details, they avoid the trauma of having to make important decisions and commitments that could drastically alter their lives. This sort of behavior, obviously, is evidence of a poor sense of perspective.

The moral is: A small businessman should learn to examine his affairs with a telescope and a microscope as well as with his own eyes.

So how do you go about acquiring perspective? It is a quality that some lucky souls seem to be born with. In lieu of being so endowed, here are a few tips that should help you achieve it.

The first is, always allow for the passage of time. A few nights' sleep does wonders for a person's point of view. What looks important to you now may seem trivial tomorrow or next week or next month. So rule number one is—procrastinate! Don't make hasty decisions when major issues are involved. Always sleep on it first.

Second, be sure to take a vacation once in a while. Many small businessmen become so tied down to their businesses that they travel in ruts. You should regularly try to get away from it all. Two weeks of being away from the phone in a completely different environment is guaranteed to clear up your head. Monumental insights can be obtained at the end of a fishing pole. In addition to vacations, take short breaks once in awhile. Leave the shop and go to an afternoon movie or sit on a park bench. Temporarily remove yourself from the situation. My favorite spot is a small park located on a hill overlooking town. When the bullets are whizzing thick and fast around my head, I sometimes leave the office and sit up there in my car for a half hour or so. I find that these little interludes help me retrieve some sense of equilibrium. The principle to remember is this: Perspective grows in direct proportion to the expansion of time and distance.

Third, always have someone outside of your own business with whom you can talk things over. There is a huge big world out there. Keeping in touch with it will help put your own affairs into perspective. As Coach John McKay once said, "400 Million Chinese could care less whether or not USC wins the Rose Bowl." So find people removed from your own personal situation whom you can chat with. Just hearing your own thoughts expressed out loud can be helpful. It may be your bartender, your C.P.A., your banker, or your Kiwanis buddy—just so he or she is not emotionally involved with your own personal problems.

Fourth, laugh. Laugh often and laugh loud. Humor releases tension. And it also helps create prespective. Learn to appreciate the ridiculousness of yourself and your situation. In my opinion, a person's sense of humor is the best indicator of his degree of sanity. Have you ever met a psychotic or highly neurotic person who had a well developed sense of humor? I haven't.

Closely related to the subject of perspective is the problem of not being able to establish and work toward long-range goals. Most people have enough foresight to pursue short-range goals, but long-range goal striving is a comparatively rare activity.

There are usually many, many details to be taken care of personally by the typical small business owner. It is very difficult to keep one's attention directed toward long-range goals with so many distractions during the course of a normal day. Consequently, most small businessmen wind up plodding along, one step at a time, looking at pebbles on the ground rather than for landmarks on the horizon. The long-range overview of their daily activities becomes a fourth dimensional concept. Only in moments of great trauma, like when their lives are threatened, do they ever see their lives in true perspective.

The trouble is, we live our lives in small increments. Our attention span usually lasts for only minutes at a time, sometimes for an hour or so, occasionally for as much as a whole day, and, on rare occasions, for a week or more.

Consequently, success is governed by the rules of integral calculus—the mathematics of the accumulation of many small increments. That is, success usually occurs only after the accumulation of many small incremental steps along the way. Firmly in mind long-range goals are necessary in order to create small living increments that are meaningful. Without long-range goals, our daily actions tend to become an aimless, random drift. Without long-range goals, we are liable to, some day, some year, sit down, add everything up, and discover that the sum of all our life's increments total "nothing."

Goals are important not only for the direction that they give, but also for the incentive and motivation they provide. Even the most mundane of activities becomes interesting if there is a goal connected with it. Peeling potatoes is drudgery of drudgeries but, if you are trying to set a new world's potato peeling record, it suddenly becomes an interesting science.

Big Business is well aware of the practical benefits that can be harvested from a program of goal setting. Big Business considers the establishment of goals as an extremely necessary management tool. Small businessmen, on the other hand, tend to regard goal setting as an abstract concept. This is unfortunate. Goals are a very useful technique.

The act of setting goals, however, needs to be a conscious, premeditated activity. It is something that you actually have to force yourself to sit down and do. Unfortunately, most small businessmen become so harried during the course of a day that they don't think about such things naturally.

From a practical standpoint, three things need to occur before a long-range goal becomes an effective motivator:

1. The goal has to be one that will provide you with something that you psychologically want very, very badly.

2. You have to be capable of vividly imagining what it would be like if you actually attained your goal.

3. You have to deep down inside sincerely believe that your goal is attainable.

The important thing to remember, though, is that for most people the process of setting a goal is something that has to be consciously and willfully done. Discipline yourself to periodically think about your goals. Make it a thinking habit. It is best to analyze your goals in writing. Getting them down on a pad of paper helps make the process less abstract. In addition, putting your thoughts in writing helps you to recognize conflicts and establish priorities. Then, periodically take your list out and review and revise it. A lot of people may feel foolish or silly doing this sort of thing, but take my word for it—it works.

9

The Art of
Being Unreasonable

Human reason is like a drunken man on horseback;
set it up on one side, and it tumbles over on the
other.

Martin Luther

It is often advantageous for a small businessman to act
unreasonably. The reason is simple.

Many times a small businessman is in the position of being an
adversary. He must engage in hassles and negotiations with
employees, with revenue agents, with suppliers, with customers,
with banks, with governmental agencies, and with competitors.
Most such negotiations involve a certain amount of give and take.
That is, each side usually grants a few concessions in order to
arrive at a settlement.

You, the small businessman, will be seeking lower wages, less
taxes, lower purchase prices, higher sales prices, more advantageous delivery schedules, better bank terms, less governmental
restrictions, less competition, and so forth and so on. Your
business adversaries will be seeking just the opposite.

Now, in most affairs of man, when two individuals negotiate from opposite points of view they usually arrive at some sort of a middle-ground compromise. For example, suppose Smith and Jones are arguing over a particular issue. Suppose that Smith's position on the particular issue at stake is at point A and that Jones' position is at point B. Suppose further that, from the point of view of each individual's best interest, the position taken by each is reasonable.

Smith and Jones will undoubtedly wind up settling their dispute somewhere between their reasonable but opposing positions. The greatest probability is that their compromise will be located somewhere near the middle. This can be shown by the following chart:

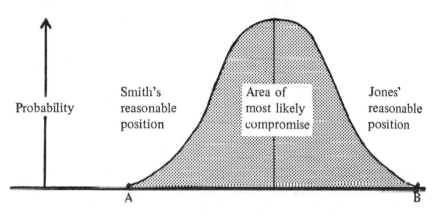

Once they have taken their respective positions, Smith and Jones will proceed to negotiate and bargain until each determines where the other's ultimate position lies. After this has been determined, they will then try to arrive at a compromise. Their compromise may fall close to A or it may fall close to B, but, based on normal probability frequency distribution curves, it will most likely fall near the middle point between positions A and B.

This is why it is, for example that judges often make decisions in court cases on the basis of a 50-50 split right down the middle between plaintiff and defendant.

This mechanism operates in practically all potential compromise situations and this is why *un*reasonableness can often be of great benefit to you. The following chart shows how an unreasonable position can help its perpetrator. Suppose that Smith, instead of taking a reasonable position at point A, takes an *un*reasonable position at point X. If Smith now argues the cause of his unreasonable point X position as convincingly as he would his reasonable point A position, then he should be able to stretch the compromise probability curve in his direction, as follows:

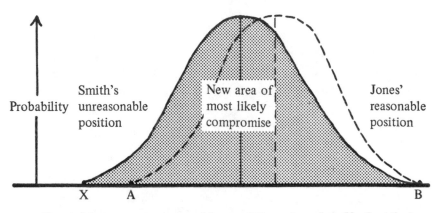

By taking an unreasonable position at point X, Smith has increased his chances of getting a more favorable compromise. In actual individual cases, Smith's compromise may still fall between A and B and it may still be closer to B than to A, but, by taking an unreasonable stance, Smith brings the probabilities more in his favor. The ultimate compromise will much more likely be closer to A than it will be to B. Such are the facts of life in the art of negotiation.

However, to make unreasonableness work in this manner, you must always be sure of one thing—that your opponent does not know that you know that your position is unreasonable. When you take an unreasonable position, you know that you are being unreasonable and chances are that your opponent knows that you are being unreasonable, *but* if your opponent *knows* that *you* know that you are being unreasonable, then all is lost. Your opponent will simply ignore your unreasonable point X position and treat you as though you are standing at point A instead. Thus your unreasonableness will not stretch the compromise distribution curve.

So, to make unreasonableness work, you must be a good actor. You must be good at the bluff. For most people, this takes practice and study.

In the course of my C.P.A. practice, I have had occasion to be exposed to many unreasonable people. After years of observing them, I have developed a few tips that should help you become a more successful unreasonable person.

Be Congenial, Courteous, and Nice

If you behave in an obnoxious and antagonistic manner, you will only succeed in arousing your opponent's emotions to the point where he will refuse to react reasonably to your unreasonableness. He may even go so far as to cut off his nose to spite his face and withdraw from further negotiations. By being a "nice," albeit unreasonable guy, you will keep him on the defensive. If he gets mad at you because of your unreasonableness, he will immediately start to feel guilty because nobody feels comfortable getting mad at a "nice" guy.

Don't Let Your "Body Language" Give You Away

Keep a straight, earnest face; avoid nervous mannerisms; adopt a self-righteous demeanor; and keep calm. It is absolutely essential that you not give your opponent any hint that you know that you are being unreasonable. If you physically give any indication that you realize you are on shaky ground, then your opponent will immediately begin to suspect the truth—that you are only bluffing.

Concede Small Issues at the Beginning
So As to Appear Reasonable

This again puts your opponent on the defensive. At the same time, it makes it seem as though you are trying to be reasonable and trying to reach a compromise.

Don't Concede Any of Your
Opponent's Points, However, Without a Fight

The objective here is to wear him down. Make him work for every small concession on your part just as though it were a major issue at stake. The more emotionally worn out your opponent becomes, the more concessions you are likely to obtain from him.

Create False Issues

Try to keep your opponent off the main issues that you are being unreasonable about. By putting forth baseless accusations and assertions, you will draw your opponent's fire and cause him to tilt with windmills. This also tends to wear him out and makes it appear that you are being reasonable when you concede, after much arguing, that you were wrong on these points.

Avoid Specifics

Try to generalize your arguments as much as possible. It is much harder to refute generalizations than it is specifics. For example, if you are arguing with a supplier, come out with something like, "Boy, it sure is hard to get deliveries from you on time. I lost lots of business last year because I didn't get your stuff soon enough to sell."

Generalizations:
—What's the definition of "hard"?
—"On time" vs. specific dates.
—How *much* business actually was lost?
—Why weren't the supplier's goods received? Were they ordered late? Was there a strike?
—Would the goods have been sold even if they had arrived timely?

Don't Lie As to Specifics

It is easy to check out basic specific facts. If you lie about them and are caught, it puts you on the defensive and discredits your whole unreasonable stance. If you are scrupulously truthful about specific facts, it lends credence to all of the other unreasonable things that you say.

Allow Your Opponent Some Room in Which to Save Face

It is much easier to get concessions out of a person if, on the surface, it appears that he is also getting concessions from you. Therefore, build up any concessions you give the other side regardless of how trivial or hollow they may be. I sat in on some negotiations once where there was a dispute between two partners in a joint venture as to the terms and conditions of their participation. One of the partners was a very tough negotiator and the other was very weak. Practically all of the major concessions were made by the weak negotiator.

Finally, after about two hours of getting nothing but his own way, the tougher partner slumped back in his chair, sighed, and said, "Well, I guess I've got no choice. You've got me over a barrel. I guess I'll just have to go along with this." The weak negotiator visibly brightened and agreed to the so-called settlement. He had given ground on every major point but he went along with it all because his tougher opponent allowed him to save face.

Acting unreasonably undoubtedly goes against the grain of everything that you've ever been taught before. Unreasonableness is one of our country's most universally frowned upon behaviorisms. The fact that this is so, however, is good. The prevalence of a predisposition towards reason in this country is exactly what enables one to capitalize on being the opposite.

In many other cultures of the world, a person is expected to act unreasonably while negotiating or bargaining. In these places it has become such a common behavior pattern that it no longer contains a competitive advantage. It merely keeps bargainers even with their competitors. In America, however, there still seems to be a bountiful supply of reasonable people to be taken advantage of, although, admittedly, it appears that their species is on the decline.

10

Sex and the
Small Businessman

*"I think 't's bad for our young people to see
all that sex going unpunished."*

A good many people fool around a little at one time or another, according to Kinsey. From what I've seen, businessmen do a pretty good job of holding up their end of the statistics. If it's possible you personally might seek extracurricular sex, one bit of advice: Stay sway from employees. Having an affair with your secretary can be bad for your business.

First of all, she won't be much good as a secretary any more. If she puts out in the bedroom, chances are she won't bother putting out much at the office. Not only that, but you will get less work out of your other employees as well. It won't take them long to figure out what is going on. You think that they won't be jealous and resentful when your lover-secretary all of a sudden moves up from the bottom of the organization chart to the top?

Love affairs with employees often lead to proprietary possessiveness. You are liable to wind up getting a new business partner as well as a new lover. Since you are sharing some of her assets, it is quite natural for her to conclude that she should be sharing some of yours. This sort of relationship very probably brought about the first implementation of the profit sharing concept.

Secretaries usually come to know a great deal about the personal side of your business, the sorts of things you would appreciate being kept confidential—your personal financial status, for example. You will undoubtedly come to regret any intimacies that you shared with her when that inevitable day arrives when the two of you break up. I shouldn't have to remind you that broken love affairs can cause intense feelings on the woman's side—a woman scorned, and all that. Mad, emotionally hurt women can turn into incredible blabbermouths. Jilted lovers, for example, are one of the biggest sources of tips the Internal Revenue Service has. In addition, there is always the unfortunate possibility that she may wind up working for a competitor. Worse yet, she may even, in a fit of pique, call up and spill the beans to your wife.

Many's the fine business that I've seen suffer because it's owner became romantically involved with an employee. An attractive employee's close proximity is a strong temptation, granted, but take my advice: If you're going to play around, do it in someone else's ball park.

11

Accounting
for Non-Accountants

The thing about accounting that you have to remember is that it is supposed to provide information that is useful to somebody.

Professor Lauren Walker

One of the factors most frequently found in small business failures is the lack of adequate accounting records. All too often an entrepreneur's discovery that he is in financial trouble is belated. It turns out that poor accounting records kept him operating in dark so that he found out too late that he was slipping over the precipice. Poor accounting records are a common occurence in small business because accounting is usually the first thing that a small businessman puts off in the heat and battle of day-to-day survival.

On the other hand, excessively elaborate record keeping systems are also a mistake. An accounting system that is too complicated inevitably breaks down and all the paperwork it creates turns out to be a chaotic, meaningless mess. This causes a small businessman to, again, wind up flying blind.

The important thing to keep in mind with respect to small business accounting systems is the art of compromise. An incomplete system is better than no system, a partial answer is better than no answer, and 50 % accuracy is better than zero accuracy.

So be sure to *have* an accounting system in your business but, for Gawd's sake, keep it simple. Installing a sophisticated accounting system in a small business is like turning a 747 airplane over to a tribe of New Guinea headhunters. That airplane won't fly without qualified pilots and mechanics to go along with it. Neither will a sophisticated accounting system work without qualified accountants and bookkeepers to work it. Most small businessmen really don't appreciate this.

"What we need around here is a better system; something that will give us accurate figures—on time!" Every small businessman who has ever lived has said these words at one time or another. When I was a young, ambitious C.P.A., I used to pounce on the chance to respond to such utterances by clients. I would set up textbook systems—vouchers, journals, subledgers, cost accounting, budgets, etc.—the works. It was always a shock to me when my clients would call back about six months later, "What the *!*! did you do to us anyway? Our old system was better than this! At least before we had *some* figures; now we've got nothing but garbage!"

Right on! How can you possibly expect to have any figures when there's nobody but dum-dums doing the figuring? My accounting systems exceeded the capacities of the personnel available for their implementation.

Good accounting personnel are hard to find. When it comes to job glamour, bookkeeping lies several fathoms below being an airplane stewardess. An accountant's life somehow doesn't quite compare to that of a secretary-tweaking, expense account living salesman. There is no C.P.A. equivalent to Perry Mason or Marcus Welby on T.V. The profession's drab image means that a whole lot of people are not knocking down doors to become accountants and bookkeepers. Lack of supply causes good ones to be hard to come by—and they are expensive. Most small businessmen can't, or won't, afford what it costs to have them. Consequently, small business accounting personnel are usually either incompetent, inexperienced, or nonexistent.

Accounting, surprisingly enough, requires a certain amount of skill and talent. You can't convert a secretary overnight into a bookkeeper, you can't turn a bookkeeper overnight into an accountant, and you can't expect one person to competently perform the functions of an entire accounting department. Most small businessmen just don't understand this. There is a tendency for them to regard an accountant as being some kind of a low-grade wizard. Give him a basket full of papers and receipts, have him wave his magic wand over the mess, and zot!—instant financial statements will appear. There aren't many accountants who can actually do this.

Big businesses get around the problem by restricting their people to specialized, repetitive tasks and by having elaborate, computerized systems involving cross checks and internal controls. With their size, they can afford to be organized in this manner. Don't expect to be able to have the same setup, though, if you are small. Big firm systems require many bodies, expensive computers, and some real sharp people at the top monitoring and supervising the whole thing.

A certain amount of accounting, however, is possible even if you are small. Whatever you have, it has to be enough to satisfy the requirements of the Internal Revenue Service. You can't get by, as one taxpayer recently tried to do in Tax Court, by claiming you have such a fantastic memory that you don't need any records. The I.R.S. gets rather stuffy when they find that your records are "not adequate to reasonably reflect your income." When this happens, they wind up estimating your taxable income using such things as bank deposits and your standard of living as guides. The only trouble is they always estimate your income on the high side in order to protect the government's interest. They also tack on plenty of penalties and interest for good measure.

Besides I.R.S. requirements, a certain amount of accounting is useful, believe it or not, in managing your business. Most small businesses wind up being run essentially by the seat of the owner's pants. Small business owners become so familiar with the details of their operations that they think they can tell without seeing any figures whether or not they are making money. Seat of the pants management, however, can be very deceptive. It's a wise seat of the pants operator who knows his true costs. Practically every time I prepare a financial statement for a client showing a loss I get the same reaction, "Well, I knew I lost money last month all right, but sure didn't realize I lost that much."

It is completely beyond the scope of this book to make an accountant out of you, even if it were possible—which it isn't. However, I do want to educate you as to a few general accounting concepts—things that you should know if you are going to manage your business intelligently. Accounting may be a pain in the neck, like washing the dishes or mowing the lawn, but it is a necessary evil. So bear with me and don't skip the rest of this chapter.

Single Entry vs. Double Entry Bookkeeping

Single entry bookkeeping is where, like the title says, you just make one entry on your books for every transaction. For example, after adding up your cash register sales for the day, you simply write down that amount in your sales journal: Tuesday, May 12, Sales $364. At the end of the month you add up the daily sales you've listed. That total is your sales for the month. At the end of the year, you add up the month's sales to get the year's total. You do the same thing for expenses—you merely list things as they occur.

Simple enough, but there is a big, fat problem with Single Entry. It is frightfully easy to make mistakes. For example, maybe your sales for the day were really $634 but you transposed the amount to $364 when you wrote it down. Or maybe you made a mistake in addition when totaling the sales for the day. Or you may even have forgotten to write the day's sales down. Anywhere along the line you may error in totaling. The bad part is that if any of these mistakes are, in fact made, they will probably never come to light. Being single entry, there is nothing to check yourself against other than by simply redoing every entry. Single entry is frowned upon by the I.R.S. and for good reason. It is not reliable—it is too easy to make mistakes.

Double entry bookkeeping was invented by Phoenician merchants to overcome this deficiency. With the double entry system, you make two offsetting entries—a debit and a credit. When you credit sales for $364.00, you also debit cash or accounts receivable the same amount. The rule is that the total debits must equal the total credits. This system smokes out the mistakes previously mentioned. If you boo-boo with the accrual system, either your books will be out of balance (the debits won't equal the credits) or else the cash and accounts receivable per your books won't agree with your bank account or your detailed accounts receivable list.

Many small businesses start out with single entry book-keeping either because of its simplicity or because they don't know any better. This is a mistake. Get started right—use double entry.

Cash vs. Accrual Accounting

Cash method accounting is where you record transactions only when they involve cash. Your accounting is composed essentially of an analysis of cash receipts and disbursements. The only other item normally recorded is depreciation of equipment and buildings.

Accrual method accounting is where you also record non-cash items such as accounts receivable, accounts payable, inventories, work in progress, prepaid expenses, and accrued liabilities.

Like single entry bookkeeping, cash method accounting is often used by small businesses because of its simplicity. The accrual method involves much more work and considerably more accounting talent. Unfortunately, cash method accounting is usually not adequate. It can be very misleading. Consider the following example:

Beginning cash	$5,000
Cash received from sales	4,000
Materials paid for	(5,000)
Others expenses paid for	(3,000)
Ending cash	$1,000
Decrease in cash and cash loss	($4,000)

Looks pretty grim, doesn't it? If you owned this business, you would be concerned, would't you? Now, let's see how this same statement looks using the accrual method.

Decrease in cash (same as in previous	
cash basis statement)	($4,000)
Increase in accounts receivable	6,000
Increase in inventory	2,000
Increase in accounts payable	(1,000)
Total increase in assets and accrual method profit . .	$3,000

The real situation is a $3,000 profit, whereas the cash method books showed a $4,000 loss! This is why cash method accounting is not a very good system. It can be misleading because it only tells part of the story. The I.R.S. frowns on cash accounting and permits it only in those businesses that do not have inventories—the so-called service businesses such as doctors, lawyers, barber shops, laundrys, etc. Even those businesses that do qualify for cash accounting often use it only for tax reporting purposes. Internally they often use accrual accounting to get a more accurate picture of what is going on.

Accrual accounting is more complicated, at least to a non-accountant. To utilize it you need such things as sales and accounts receivable journals, accounts payable journals, and perpetual inventory records. You can, however, take a few shortcuts. Keep your regular books on the cash method—record only cash receipts and disbursements. Then, when it comes time to prepare a financial statement, simply inventory your accrual account items—meaning your receivables, payables and inventory. Add them to your balance sheet figures and add the changes in them from the beginning of the year to your income statement figures. You then have statements prepared on the accrual method. This is an oversimplified explanation, naturally, but for your purposes it is the general idea that counts. Seek professional help for details.

By now you are probably saying, "All right, wise guy, at the beginning of this chapter you said to keep everything simple. But so far all you've done is shoot down the simplest way of keeping books—single entry, cash accounting." True, but what I said was to keep it simple—not ridiculous. Single entry cash accounting is almost no accounting at all.

Bookkeeping vs. Accounting

You may have noticed that I keep using two terms in this chapter—"bookkeeping" and "accounting." These are not synonyms. There is a difference between the two and it is important that you know what it is.

Bookkeeping is the process of recording details. Bookkeepers are the ones who have the chore of recording and entering individual transactions into journals and subledgers. They also prepare many of the documents pertaining to original sources of entry—invoices, vouchers, checks, receipts, etc.

Accounting is the process of putting it all together. Accountants enter journal totals and other figures accumulated by bookkeepers into the general ledger. They analyze and adjust the various accounts, draw up financial reports, and prepare tax returns. Accountants are responsible for coordinating and integrating the flow of financial information into its final resting place—the financial statements. Accounting is higher level stuff. It requires more training and background than bookkeeping.

Many small businessmen are unaware of this distinction. They try to have bookkeepers do the work of accountants and vice versa. They hire some bookkeeper with 15 years' experience maintaining an accounts receivable ledger and expect her to come up with accurate monthly financial statements. Or they hire a highly qualified accountant and expect him to spend his time preparing checks and running the bookkeeping machine. Actually you need both. If your business is small, you can usually get by having a full-time bookkeeper on the premises with an outside professional accountant coming in periodically for the general ledger work and preparation of financial statements. Eventually, as you grow larger, a full-charge, in-house accountant will be warranted.

Cost Accounting

Imagine that you are a small general contractor and that you have two jobs going. One is the construction of a duplex. The other is a remodeling job on a small office building. Suppose further that your financial statements show the following:

Gross income from jobs	$10,000
Labor costs	(3,000)
Materials and supplies costs	(3,000)
Gross profit before overhead	$4,000

Now it would be nice to know how much of the $4,000 gross profit is attributable to each job, wouldn't it? I mean suppose you are losing money on one and making all your profit on the other? If you knew this, you might still have a chance to salvage the loser and turn it around while it is still in process. Also, you would probably alter your estimates the next time a job similar to the loser came up for bidding.

Or suppose you are in light manufacturing and you produce several products. Your financial statements might show a profit overall but it would be very useful to know how much profit each individual product contributed. Such information would influence your sales efforts and probably cause you to seek ways of cutting costs on the low margin items.

This is what cost accounting is all about. You can't tell the players without a program.

Cost accounting is simple in theory. All you do is classify individual costs into two categories instead of just one. An invoice from Ajax Lumber Company for $500 would be classified: "Materials, $500, Job 101." The total material expense for the month is then broken down and subtotalled by individual job numbers. The same thing is done with labor and supplies.

As you can see, cost accounting involves a lot more bookkeeping. You have to classify every expense by job or product number as well as by major expense category. In addition, not all costs are so neatly categorized. Suppose you, the contractor, have a truck running around on your two jobs in process. How do you allocate its costs of operation between the two jobs? What about repairs to equipment? How about shop supplies expense? A certain amount of arbitrary allocating becomes necessary. Then there is the problem of balancing the costs allocated to the various individual jobs with the total expense categories in the general ledger. The whole thing gets rather complicated after awhile. But don't be discouraged. Cost accounting is a very powerful tool, even it it only accounts for direct costs. In certain businesses it is absolutely essential—in construction and manufacturing, obviously, and any business where work is done on a bid basis.

Bookkeeping Systems

There are six basic bookkeeping systems:

1. Manual
2. One-write, or pegboard
3. Bookkeeping machines
4. Punched card equipment
5. Computers
6. Computer service bureaus

Most small businesses use manual bookkeeping. It is the simplest and most flexible system. Individual transactions are merely listed by hand in journals. The journal totals are then posted by hand to the general ledger. Having to write everything in long hand breaks down, of course, when you get to the point where there are a great many entries to make. Therefore, many businesses eventually go to some form of a one-write system, at least for part of their bookkeeping.

One-write systems are a form of manual posting also but by using carbon paper and a special writing board you make the same entry on several different pieces of paper at the same time. Take sales invoicing for example. Normally, when you list a sales invoice you have to record it in three different places—the sale journal, the customer's accounts receivable card, and the customer's monthly statement. Each is a separate posting. With a one-write system, however, one posting records the invoice simultaneously in all three places. The same thing can be done with cash receipts, payroll, and cash disbursements. One-write systems not only save you posting time, they also cut down on posting errors. The use of the carbon paper insures that you post the same figures in all three places.

The next step up is to go to some form of a bookkeeping machine. Bookkeeping machines do the same things one-write systems do—that is, they create multiple postings in one pass. Bookkeeping machines have wide carriages so that two or three forms can be simultaneously posted. In addition, they automatically total the entries being posted. The more elaborate machines even perform calculations such as payroll tax computations or sales invoice extensions.

Punched card equipment is the old familiar IBM card, plus the equipment used to prepare and process it. Having your accounting in the form of IBM cards gives you the capacity to handle quite a bit of detail. In addition, punched cards are a more flexible system than bookkeeping machines. Once information is in the form of an IBM card, it becomes possible to process it or list it any number of different ways.

Even a bookkeeping machine or a punched card system breaks down if you try to process too many entries. Then you have to go to some form of computerized bookkeeping. Computers do the same things bookkeeping machines and punched card equipment do except they do more of it and they do it a lot faster. Once original entries are cranked into a computer, your accounting becomes pretty much automated. If it's programmed properly, a computer can be a fabulous tool. It can eliminate lots of drudgery and produce more financial information than you can shake a stick at. *If* it's programmed properly. And *if* it's fed the proper information. When something is fed into the maw of a computer, it had better be accurate. Otherwise you'll pay hell straightening out the ensuing mess coming out the other end.

There is one other system available. Instead of buying a computer, you can hire someone else already owning a computer to process your stuff for you. Companies that do this for a living are known as "Service Bureaus." They take your source docu ments, which you have previously coded and classified, and process them through their computers. Theoretically, this is a good system. You have the advantages of a computer but not the expenses of owning one. There are a couple of problems, though. Half the time your source documents are at the Service Bureau just when you need them in your own office. Then there is always the communication problem. Having your accounting done outside of your office increases chances of error. Service Bureau employees don't usually understand what they are processing. They just run the stuff through the same way they receive it.

A variation of the Service Bureau concept is something called "on-line terminals." This is where you have a keyboard in your office that is connected by telephone to a Service Bureau's computer. You are then able to directly enter information from your own office into the computer. On-line terminals are a fairly new concept but they undoubtedly represent the wave of the future. Eventually, giant computers will be like utilities. Everyone will be connected to them through terminals.

The costs of the six different systems vary tremendously. Manual bookkeeping supplies should cost you less than one hundred dollars. One-write systems usually cost several hundred dollars. The costs of bookkeeping machines vary depending upon their complexity and capacity but, generally speaking, you are talking in terms of thousands of dollars.

Punched card equipment can be rented for about five hundred to a thousand dollars a month. The basic equipment can usually be purchased used for $10,000 to $20,000.

Computers also vary tremendously but at a minimum they will be in the order of tens of thousands of dollars. Computer companies have been coming out with "baby" computers for accounting applications hoping to get their prices down into the range small businesses can afford. As of this writing, however, they are still a mighty expensive item.

Service Bureau charges depend upon the volume of transactions they process. At a minimum, they should cost from $500 to $1,000 a month.

If you are going to spend money on an accounting system, the place to splurge is on your personnel. As indicated earlier, I don't care how good your system is on paper, if you've got nothing but dodos around to run it, you're bound to have a mess on your hands.

Manual systems are fine to start out with. When you grow to say, ten employees you should start thinking about a one-write system for at least part of your bookkeeping. When you get to the point where you are writing over a hundred checks a month or you have several hundred receivable accounts, you are probably in the area where a simple bookkeeping machine is warranted. Computers and punched card equipment should be reserved for those situations where transactions are running into the thousands.

Bookkeeping Hints

• The main thing is to leave lots of tracks. Have everything written down in some kind of a logical, systematic manner.

• Use checks instead of cash for every expense you can. Cancelled checks are an excellent record.

• Deposit *all* receipts in the bank. When you start keeping out some cash receipts for payment of expenses, very likely you'll get mixed up as to what your real income is.

• Use credit cards whenever possible for travel and entertainment items. The I.R.S. is very sticky about support for T & E expense. With a credit card, at least you have proof of the amount, the time, and the place. You can then probably recall from your appointment calendar who you spent it on.

• Use "control cards" for all subsidiary ledgers such as accounts receivable, employee earnings records, and accounts payable. Control cards contain the totals of the individual amounts that have been posted to the individual detail ledger cards. Balancing the detail ledgers to the control card totals enables you to more readily detect posting errors in the detail ledger cards.

• If the type of business you are in has inventories, count and price your inventory at least twice a year. This is known as taking a physical inventory. Physical inventories are necessary in order to prepare accurate financial statements. Without an accurate physical inventory the profit on your books is nothing more than an estimate.

• Pay creditors based on original invoices rather than on monthly statements. It's usually difficult reconciling your purchases with suppliers' statements, what with different posting cut-offs and all. If you base all payments on original invoices, you can't go wrong.

• When you pay an invoice, write "paid" on the face of your copy. Also, mark on it the date and the check number that you paid it with. This way you avoid the possibility of paying or processing the same invoice twice.

• Check prices, footings, quantities, and extensions on the bills that you pay. People do make mistakes and oftentimes it is in their favor. The time and trouble involved in checking your bills usually pays off. I know one businessman who claims that the errors found on his suppliers' invoices almost pay for his whole accounting department.

•Get professional help from an outside accountant before you set up your bookkeeping and accounting system. Don't be a basket case. Don't take a mixed-up box full of receipts and papers to an accountant at the end of the year and expect him to make any sense out of it.

12

Understanding the Mishmash and Gobbledegook of Financial Statements

It is likewise to be observed that this society hath a peculiar chant and jargon of their own, that no other mortal can understand, and wherein all their laws are written, which they take special care to multiply.

Jonathan Swift, *Gulliver's Travels*

Don't be embarrassed if financial statements are mysterious to you. They are meant to be. Accountants are no different than any other professional. They seek to protect their status by producing an unintelligible product. Even bankers and experienced businessmen have trouble understanding financial statements. There is just enough jargon in them to be confusing. Most people get left in the bushes by such terms as:

Current Assets—Meaning—Assets that, hopefully, will become cash within a year. Current assets consist of cash, accounts receivable, inventories, prepaid expenses, and marketable securities.

Fixed Assets—Meaning—The amount that you have paid for equipment, trucks, buildings and land. Fixed Assets are things that, hopefully, will last at least several years.

Intangible Assets—Meaning—The cost of assets that you can't touch, feel, or see. In other words, they are intangible. Usually, a piece of paper evidences their existence. Examples—costs of obtaining a patent, costs of organizing a corporation, costs of a non-competition agreement, cost of obtaining goodwill, etc.

Accumulated Depreciation—Meaning—The amount of your fixed assests that you've managed to write-off against income taxes. Depreciation is something you claim happened when talking to the tax collector but claim didn't happen when talking to a potential buyer.

Amortization—Meaning—The same thing as depreciation except it applies to intangible assets.

Allowance for Doubtful Accounts—Meaning—The amount of money owed to you by deadbeats whom you suspect aren't ever going to pay up.

Prepaid Expenses—Meaning—Expenses you've paid for but haven't used up yet. Like next month's rent paid in advance or office supplies on hand that will last a year, or insurance premiums that cover the next three years, etc.

Fifo Inventory—Meaning—"First in, first out." Fifo is the assumption that your inventory consists of the items you last purchased. In other words, that you sold your oldest inventory items first, which is smart merchandising.

Lifo Inventory—Meaning "Last in, first out." The opposite of Fifo. The assumption that your inventory consists of the same items you started out with years ago. In other words, that your most recent inventory acquisitions are what you sell first. You hope like hell that this doesn't actually happen but it is a good assumption to make for tax purposes. During times of inflation, which is always, valuing your inventory at old costs reduces taxable income.

Current Liabilities—Meaning—The liabilities you owe that will have to be paid off within one year. Accounts payable, short-term bank notes, accrued taxes, one year's payments on mortgages, etc.

Accrued Liabilities—Meaning—Money that you owe people but haven't been billed for yet. Examples—utility bills, property taxes, income tax withheld on salaries, accumulated interest on promissory notes, etc. You might like to forget about them but you know that they won't forget about you so you face the music and accrue them while waiting for the actual bills to arrive.

Contingent Liabilities—Meaning—Debts and obligations you may get stuck with but only if you are unlucky—like your brother-in-law's bank loans that you have co-signed. Your liability on them is contingent upon whether or not he lives up to your suspicions of his being a deadbeat.

Working Capital—Meaning—The difference between your current assets and current liabilities. This is the amount of cash that would be left over if you paid off all of your current bills. Working capital is something that it is nice to have lots of.

Deferred Credits—Meaning—Money you've received but haven't earned yet, or being paid in advance for services to be performed later.

Paid-in Capital—Meaning—The amount of money stock-holders put into their corporation in addition to the par value of their capital stock.

Cost of Goods Sold—Meaning—The direct costs of producing or acquiring whatever it is that you sell: Materials, if you are a retailer; materials and labor, if you are a contractor; materials, labor and factory overhead, if you are a manufacturer.

Retained Earnings—Meaning—The amount of net profit that your business has earned over the years that you haven't yet taken out in the form of salary or dividends

As you can see, it's much simpler to use these terms than it is to write down the explanations associated with them. Accounting terminology is a form of shorthand. It's something you have to live with awhile before it connotes real meaning.

Once you get used to the special language and the format, financial statements aren't all that hard to understand—at least, not small business financial statements. Here is an example of one for the fictitious Doozy Mfg. Co., simplified and boiled down to its essentials:

THE DOOZY MFG. CO.
BALANCE SHEET

Assets

Cash	$ 5,000
Receivables	70,000
Inventory	13,000
Building & Equipment	47,000
Total Assets	$135,000

Liabilities

Accounts payable	$ 48,000
Bank Note	15,000
Building & Equipment Mortgages	27,000
Total Liabilities	$ 90,000

Net Worth	45,000
Total Liabilities and Net Worth	$135,000

THE DOOZY MFG. CO.
INCOME STATEMENT

Sales	$300,000
Cost of Goods Sold	200,000
Gross Profit	$100,000

Overhead Expenses

Bad debts	12,000
Depreciation	4,000
Interest Expense	2,000
Office Expense	1,000
Taxes	5,000
Truck Expense	7,000
Utilities & Maintenance	4,000
Wages & Salaries	45,000
	$ 80,000

Net Profit Before Owner's Salary	$ 20,000
Owner's Salary	15,000
Net Profit	$ 5,000
Net Worth at Beginning of Year	40,000
Net Worth at End of Year	$ 45,000

First of all, notice that there are two parts to Doozy's financial statement:

1. The Balance Sheet—which tells you where you are; and,
2. The Income Statement—which tells you how you've been doing.

The Balance Sheet tells you what your assets, liabilities, and net worth are at a given point in time. The Income Statement tells you how much money you have made and how you made it.

Once you have financial statements, it becomes important to know how to use them. Using financial statements is a three-step process:

1. First you figure out what happened;
2. Next, you try to figure out why it happened;
3. Finally, you figure out what, if anything, to do about it.

To accomplish these things, you need some basis of comparison and you need to know the relationships between accounts. To have comparisons, the thing to do is to line up last year's figures beside this year's figures. To establish relationships, compute the percentage that each expense is to sales. Doing these things to Doozy Mfg. Co.'s financial statements makes them look like this:

THE DOOZY MFG. CO.
COMPARATIVE BALANCE SHEET
(In thousands of dollars)

Assets	This Year	Last Year	Increase (Decrease)
Cash	$ 5	$ 15	$(10)
Receivables	70	30	40
Inventory	13	10	3
Building & Equipment	47	45	2
Total Assets	$135	$100	$ 35
Liabilities			
Accounts payable	$ 48	$ 17	$ 31
Bank Notes	15	10	5

Building & Equipment			
Mortgages	27	33	(6)
Total Liabilities	$ 90	$ 60	$ 30
Net Worth	45	40	5
	$135	$100	$ 35

THE DOOZY MFG. CO.
COMPARATIVE INCOME STATEMENT
(In thousands of dollars)

	This Year		Last Year	
	$	%	$	%
Sales	$300	100%	$240	100%
Cost of Goods Sold	200	67	143	60
Gross Profit	$100	33%	$ 97	40%
Overhead Expenses:				
Bad Debts	$ 12	4%	$ 6	3%
Depreciation	4	1	5	2
Interest Expense	2	1	4	2
Office Expense	1	—	2	—
Taxes	5	2	4	2
Truck Expense	7	2	9	4
Utilities & Maintenance	4	1	5	2
Wages	45	15	40	16
Total	$ 80	26%	$ 75	31%
Net Profit Before Owner's Salary	$ 20	7	$ 22	9
Owner's Salary	15	5	15	6
Net Profit	$ 5	2%	$ 7	3%
Net Worth at Beginning of Year	40		33	
Net Worth at End of Year	$ 45		$ 40	

As you can see, these statements give us a lot more to work with. Now, how is Doozy Mfg. Co. doing and where can it stand improvement?

Well, first of all, this year's profit is $5,000. That amounts to only 2% of sales for the year. Seems like a pretty thin profit margin doesn't it? But that isn't the percentage that is important.

What counts is the percent of profit made on the dollars invested in the business. In other words, what was Doozy's return on his investment? Doozy's net worth at the beginning of the year was $40,000. With this investment he earned a profit of $5,000. This means he made 12-1/2% return on his money ($5,000 ÷ $40,000).

This year's net profit, however, is $2,000 less than last year's. Even though sales increased 25% from $240,000 to $300,000, profits dropped. This is bad. What could have caused decreased profits on increased sales? For one thing, cost-of-goods-sold jumped up from 60% to 67% of sales. If cost-of-goods-sold had stayed at 60%, Doozy would have had another $20,000 profit this year. Probably one of two things happened. Either Doozy is now paying more for labor and materials, in which case he had better think about raising prices; or else, his manufacturing was more inefficient, in which case Doozy had better hustle out into his plant and find out what is going on.

Overhead expenses increased by $5,000 over last year. That is a 7% increase. Sales increased 25% so the 7% increase in overhead doesn't look too far out of line. Overhead expenses are the types of things that shouldn't vary much with sales. Ideally they should remain relatively constant from one period to another.

In looking over specific overhead items, however, we see that bad debts are 4% of sales. This is a high percentage. It is even higher than Doozy's net profit margin. Doozy had better tighten up on his credit and collection procedures.

Bankers and credit men place great stock in a business' Current Asset Ratio. This is the ratio between current assets (assets that will be turned into cash within one year) and current liabilities (liabilities that must be paid within one year). If you have a Current Asset Ratio of 2 to 1 or more, the banker considers you to be in good shape. If your Current Asset Ratio ever gets down to 1 to 1, you are in serious trouble. Doozy's current assets are $88,000 (cash and receivables and inventory). Current liabilities are $63,000 (accounts payable and bank note). This is a 1.4 to 1 ratio which is nothing to brag about. Last year's Current Asset Ratio was 2 to 1. If Doozy's current ratio keeps declining at this same rate, he will soon be in trouble.

It appears as though Doozy may have too much money tied up in receivables. His customers owe him $70,000 and this is equal to 61 days' sales.

$$\frac{\dfrac{\$70,000 \text{ receivables}}{\$300,000 \text{ sales}}}{260 \text{ business days}} = 61 \text{ days}$$

If he had kept his receivables down to last year's level—which was 33 days' sales—he would have had another $31,918 of cash to reduce his payables by. That would have made his Current Assets Ratio 1.8 to 1. What with both a high bad debt ratio and a high level of receivables, it is clear that Doozy is soft on collections.

Now, back up a minute.

Remember in the foregoing analysis where we figured out Doozy's return on his investment? It was:

$$\frac{\$5,000 \text{ profit}}{\$40,000 \text{ Net Worth}} = 12\text{-}1/2\%$$

That was a very important calculation. Return on your investment, after all, is what it is all about. Large, publicly held corporations try like mad to increase their earnings per share of stock every year. Paradoxically, small businessmen hardly ever think in these terms. They characteristically tangle themselves up in so many details that they never take the time to stand back to see what rate of return they are making on the investment that they have in their business.

However, the way we calculated Doozy's return was misleading. We assumed in our equation that the figures on Doozy's books represented true values. Actually, this is hardly ever the case. Doozy's building and equipment show up on his books as being $47,000. But that is not what they are really worth. Book figures merely represent what the assets originally cost minus whatever depreciation has been written off.

The amount of depreciation written off is an artificial figure. It very seldom, if ever, represents true economic depreciation. Especially where real estate is concerned. What with inflation and expanding population, real estate usually appreciates rather than depreciates. Equipment, on the other hand, often depreciates faster than what the books show. Here is what Doozy's schedule of fixed assets looks like comparing current market values to original costs:

	Original Cost	Less Accumulated Depreciation	Equals the Value on Doozy's Books	Whereas the Actual Values are:
Buildings and Land	$50,000	($13,000)	$37,000	$60,000
Equipment	20,000	(10,000)	10,000	7,000
	$70,000	($23,000)	$47,000	$67,000

In other words, the value of Doozy's fixed assets is really $20,000 more than what his books show. This means that Doozy's net worth is $20,000 greater. In terms of actual values, it is $60,000, not $40,000. Therefore, Doozy's real rate of return is:

$$\frac{\$5,000 \text{ Profit}}{\$60,000 \text{ Net Worth}} = 8\text{-}1/3\%$$

Based on what Doozy's assets are really worth, he is only making 8% rather than 12%.

What I'm trying to illustrate here is that you can't necessarily take financial statements at their face value. They may contain hidden assets, as in Doozy's case. Or, conversely, assets may be overstated. Accounts receivable, for example, may include unrecognized bad debts. Inventories may be inaccurate. Some bills may have been left off accounts payable.

The small business owner may have included personal assets on his balance sheet. His boat and camper may be included in "equipment." He may be including his girlfriend on the payroll. He may be writing off other personal living expenses as "overhead." He may be renting a building to his corporation but at an unrealistic rental rate. All sorts of distortions and inaccuracies are possible, particularly in small businesses where controls and accounting talent are normally weak.

If you're serious about analyzing a financial statement, you must be aware of these things. One device used to make financial statements more accurate is to have an audit done. This is where an outside C.P.A. performs certain elaborate audit steps designed to ensure the correctness of the final figures. Audits, however, are very expensive. For this reason, small businesses rarely have them done. This is why most small business financial statements have "Prepared without Audit" typed on them.

"Prepared without Audit" means that, although the C.P.A. prepared the statements, he did not do the audit steps necessary to be able to professionally certify that they reasonably represent the business' financial position.

The Securities and Exchange Commission requires that all publicly held corporations have annual audits. Small businesses, though, are audited only on special occasions because of the high cost involved. Banks and bonding companies sometimes require audits before they will loan or bond a business. Often audits are performed when a business is being sold. Usually though, the owner will have to double-check his statements himself for accuracy.

Half of the time, when I show a business owner a profitable financial statement, he says something like, "Whad'ya mean I had $XX,XXX profit? If I made that much money, where is it?" Unless his profit shows up in the form of cash in the till, he has trouble believing that it actually exists. To solve this problem, a third form of financial statement has become very popular. It's called, "Changes in Financial Position" or "Funds Statement." Audited statements always have a Funds Statement presented along with the traditional Balance Sheet and Income Statement. Funds Statements haven't quite caught on yet in the world of small business, but undoubtedly more and more of them will be prepared in the future,

Balance Sheets, remember, tell you "what you've got" and Income Statements tell you "how much you've made." Well, Funds Statements tell you "what happened to it."

Here is a Funds Statement for Doozy Mfg. Co.:

THE DOOZY MFG. CO.
STATEMENT OF CHANGES IN FINANCIAL POSITION
(Otherwise Known as a Funds Statement)

(Thousands of
Dollars)

Doozy obtained working capital from the following sources:

From sales:

Net profit (see Income Statement)	$ 5
Add-back depreciation which is a non-cash expense and doesn't require working capital	4
	$ 9

Doozy used working capital for the following purposes:

To reduce long-term mortgages	$ 6
To buy new equipment	6
	12
So that Doozy's working capital decreased by:	($ 3)

Increase/(decrease) in the elements of working capital:

Current Assets—

Decrease in cash	($10)
Increase in receivables	40
Increase in inventory	3
	$33

Current Liabilities—

Increase in accounts payable	$31
Increase in bank loans	5
	$36
Net decrease in working capital:	($ 3)

In other words, Doozy's business operations created funds of $9,000. However, Doozy used up $12,000 of funds so that he depleted his working capital by $3,000. He paid his mortgages down by $6,000 and he bought another $6,000 worth of equipment. If Doozy asks me where his profit went, I can now answer that it is tied up in new equipment and increased equity in his fixed assets. Funds Statements can be very illuminating and ought to be prepared more often.

Generally speaking, this is how you go about analyzing financial statements. They should be used as tools to help make management decisions. Too often financial statements are meaningful only to the accountant. The small business owner winds up merely looking at the bottom profit figure. I strongly advise that you learn how to understand financial statements. Their usefulness will surprise you.

13

Paperwork, Schmaperwork

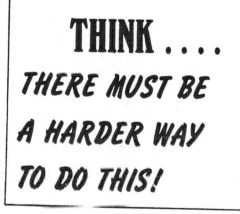

THINK....

THERE MUST BE

A HARDER WAY

TO DO THIS!

The amount of paperwork involved these days in running a small business is incredible. Here, for example, are some of the reports a typical small business client of mine is faced with:

1. Corporate income tax return.
2. State income tax return.
3. State business and occupational tax return.
4. City business and occupational tax return.
5. State unemployment tax return.
6. Federal unemployment tax return.
7. Federal unemployment tax quarterly deposits.
8. State industrial insurance report.
9. Annual state corporate license renewal.

10. Federal F.I.C.A. and withholding tax return.
11. Biweekly F.I.C.A. and witholding tax deposits.
12. Corporate quarterly estimated income tax payments.
13. Federal Bureau of the Census report.
14. Personal property tax affidavit.
15. Computation of minimum tax on tax preference items—Form 4626.
16. Annual Pension Plan Statements—Forms 4898 and 4849.
17. Union health and welfare reports (one for each union).
18. Federal employment of minorities report.
19. U.S. information return—Form 1099.
20. Annual summary of Form 1099's—Form 1096.
21. Federal highway use tax return.
22. Federal excise tax return.
23. Employees' W-2 forms.
24. Employees' W-4 forms.
25. Reconciliation of Federal income tax withheld from employees—Form W-3.
26. Application for refund of gas tax paid on non-highway use.

I've probably left some out, but this should be enough to give you the idea. In addition, it is necessary to contend with cancelled checks, bank statements, invoices, general correspondence, various bookkeeping journals, time-keeping records, purchase orders, copies of phone messages, accounting records, inventory records, suppliers' statements, contracts, the corporate minute book, petty cash receipts, etc., etc.

Just a few years of being in business are enough to create a plethora of paperwork. How in the world do you keep from being smothered by it all? Here are a few hints to help control your paperwork burden.

Records Retention

First of all, you don't have to keep all of this paperwork around forever. Some of it you do, but much of it can be thrown away after awhile. The following items should be kept indefinitely:

General ledgers.

Copies of income tax returns.

All evidences of ownership such as deeds, titles, right-of-way and easement records, copyrights, letter of patents, partnership agreements, and trademark registrations.

Formal corporate documents, such as articles of incorporation, by-laws, minutes, stock certificate books, and cancelled stock certificates.

Everything else can, sooner or later, be disposed of. The actual number of years that a particular record is kept depends upon the type of business you are in, the type of record it is, and what your state's statute of limitations is. The Internal Revenue Service has a 3-year statute of limitations. However, if your gross income is understated by 25% or more, the I.R.S. applies a 6-year statute of limitations. Consequently, you should keep most accounting records a minimum of 6 years. As to other records, you should check with your accountant and your attorney. The important thing is to set up an actual timetable for disposing of records and to periodically review it. Many people just keep accumulating records year after year. They can tell you how much pencils cost them back in 1937 but their offices are so crowded they can't find the pencils that they bought last week.

Filing

I wish I had a nickel for every minute I've spent looking for misplaced or misfiled records. Alphabetical filing is the most logical filing system. The trouble is, not every body files alphabetically the same way. Particularly secretaries. Suppose you receive a quotation on the price of some parts for Job # 101 from a Mr. Smith, the sales manager of the Charles Jones., Inc. Do you file this correspondence under—Smith? Jones? Charles? Parts? Quotations? Job # 101?

Actually, it doesn't matter what alphabetical category you use as long as it is *logical to you*. Hence: don't ever give your secretary something to file without first marking right on the document itself where you want it to be filed.

If a particular paper might be useful and logical information under more than one category, then have your secretary make extra photo copies for duplicate filing. The few pennies the extra copies cost aren't anything compared to the savings made later on by being able to put your hands on a copy when you need one.

Professional office experts advise setting up filing systems similar to the method libraries use. That is—first you establish broad categories; then you establish sub-categories within the broad categories; then you alphabetize within the sub-categories.

For example, a broad category for you might be "Sales." A subcategory within "Sales" might be "Complaints." A complaint letter from a Mrs. Painintheneck would then be filed in this order, "Sales, Complaints, Painintheneck."

Whole Dollar Accounting

When was the last time you bothered to bend over to pick up a penny lying on the ground? When was the last time you actually bought something with a penny? Pennies these days are practically worthless. As a matter of fact, they are so worthless it isn't worthwhile to keep track of them anymore.

In most businesses you can safely round off bookkeeping entries to the nearest dollar and not materially affect anything at all. Do you have any idea how much writing this saves? The average bookkeeping entry for most small businesses is usually a four digit number—$XX.XX. Not writing down the pennies means you eliminate 60% of the average entry—you eliminate the decimal point and the two penny digits.

The I.R.S. permits tax returns to be rounded off to the nearest dollar. So do most states. Financial statements should always be rounded off. You can also round off to the nearest dollar in your general ledger and in most journals.

Eliminating pennies not only cuts down on the number of digits you write, it also cuts down on mistakes. You would be surprised how many bookkeeping mistakes are made in recording pennies.

Pareto's Law

Ever hear of Pareto's Law? Don't feel bad. Neither have most other people. But you may already be intuitively aware of it.

Pareto's Law is a family of frequency distribution curves describing situations where the significant items in a group constitute only a small portion of the group's total items. Pareto's Law says, in other words, that within any given group, a few items are important, but most are unimportant.

For example: a small part of the total population owns most of the country's wealth; a few members of any club usually carry on most of the club's activities; a small percentage of salesmen create a majority of a company's total sales; a few major businesses account for most of the sales in any particular industry; and only a small percentage of inventory items make up most of an inventory's value.

Pareto's Law can be usefully applied to the following:

ABC Inventory Control System

If you analyze your inventory, chances are you'll find something like the following:

A. 10% of the items = 60% of the inventory's total value.
B. 30% of the items = 30% of the inventory's total value.
C. 60% of the items = 10% of the inventory's total value.

Now instead of trying to keep track of every single inventory item, you do this:

"A. items"—keep track of each individual item.
"B. items"—keep track of in total only and count periodically.
"C. items"—estimate and count infrequently.

In other words, you keep track of the big ticket items and don't waste your time on the nuts and bolts. Instead of creating a lot of records keeping good track of 100% of your inventory's value, you only create a small number of records to (A) keep good track of 60% of it, (B) keep reasonably good track of 30% of it, and (C) give the other 10% a lick and a promise.

Correlate Customer Traffic with Clerical Personnel

If you keep track of how many customers go through your store at various times during the day, you'll undoubtedly find that most customers come in during only a few key peak hours. If this is the case, consider cutting down on full-time employees and hiring part-time employees during peak hours only. *Example:* one very successful chain of spaghetti houses stays open only during peak dining hours, thereby getting by with only one shift of employees.

Test Check Vendors' Invoices

Instead of checking every single bill you receive, check only the ones over a certain large dollar amount. Then merely test check the smaller ones.

Trim Your Product Line

Very likely only a small number of your products account for most of your sales. Consider eliminating the small movers. Concentrate on the big sellers.

Be Selective in Sending out Monthly Customers' Statements

You'll probably find that only a few customers actually pay based on the monthly statements you send them. Instead, most customers will probably pay based on the original invoice. So why bother sending them monthly statements that they will pay no attention to? Instead, only send monthly statements to those customers that request them and to delinquent accounts as reminders that their payments are overdue. By not sending monthly statements to every single customer you will save postage, stationery, and clerical time.

One-Write Bookkeeping Systems

I've mentioned one-write, or pegboard bookkeeping systems previously. A one-write system, you will recall, is where you make multiple entries on several records by using carbon paper and a special pegboard. Being able to make several entries at one writing is a good way to cut down on your paperwork. One-write systems are the first step up for a small business from a straight manual posting system. They are particularly useful in recording payrolls and accounts receivable.

"Writ" by Hand

You'll usually save yourself considerable time if you write checks, invoices, statements, and short correspondence in longhand. Of course, handwriting doesn't look nearly as neat or nice as typing. For this reason, most small businessmen are reluctant to use handwritten documents for fear they will reflect badly on their image. Nonsense. You are running a business, not a beauty contest.

Multiple Voucher Checks

Two-part, three copy voucher checks can be handy. They look something like this:

The Doozy Co.		No. 105	
		12/1	
Payee		$100.00	
One hundred & No/100 dollars			
First Natl. Bank		The Doozy Co.	
Date	Description	Acct. No.	Amount
12/1	Supplies	680	$100.00

The bottom part of the check is used to describe what the payment is for and what accounting classification it is to be charged against. The gimmick is that each voucher check has two carbon copies attached to it. The original, or top copy, is the actual check and is what goes to the payee. One of the two carbon copies underneath is filed away in numeric order. These numerically filed copies constitute your check register and check book. The second carbon copy is filed away alphabetically, usually with a copy of the payee's invoice attached.

With this system you eliminate the necessity of posting information about the checks on check stubs or on cash disbursement journals, thus saving considerable bookkeeping time. You also have, with the multiple copies, an easy to follow record of when every bill is paid, how much of it was paid, and where the amount was charged.

Eliminate Subledgers

Another trick often used in big businesses is not keeping individual ledger accounts for either receivables or payables. Instead, unpaid bills and unpaid invoices are kept track of by merely filing them alphabetically in unpaid invoice files. When they are paid, the invoices are merely marked and transferred to a "paid" file. Not having to post and reconcile accounts receivable and accounts payable ledgers saves lots of time.

Don't rush into this kind of a system, however, until you consider the disadvantage—which is, that you can lose control of your receivables and payables by not reconciling to individual account ledgers.

Batch Your Work

Long production runs are more efficient than short production runs. Starting and stopping numerous tasks throughout the day isn't a productive way to operate, obviously.

So, whenever possible, batch your work and have your employees do the same. Try to stick with a job throughout its completion, or at least until you reach a logical stopping place.

Write and record checks at one time during the month rather than throughout the month; do your invoicing at one time; post accounts receivable at one time; do your filing at one time; do correspondence at one time; and so on.

Delegate

The most precious commodity that you possess as a small business owner is your own time. Be stingy with it. Don't spend your own time doing things that employees can do for you. Learn to delegate.

The trap many small businessmen fall into is that they become afraid of the mistakes that their employees may make, so they wind up trying to cover all the bases themselves. It is far better to tolerate some mistakes being made by employees if by so doing, it allows you time to make sure that all of your major problems are taken care of.

It should be self-evident that delegation of authority is the only way to go, unless you want to stay exceedingly small. Keep reminding yourself that this is so.

Question Your Habits

We are creatures of habit and this can be a problem. It is good every once in awhile to question yourself:

Why Am I Doing This;
Is It Necessary?
Is There a Better Way?

A small example: Federal corporation income tax returns used to have a place right next to the signature line for the placing of the corporation's seal. For years I advised my clients to put their corporate seals on their corporation income tax returns. This was usually a nuisance because most small corporations keep their seals in their attorney's office. One day a brilliant thought struck me, "Is a corporate seal *really* necessary?" Upon investigation I discovered that the only reason the I.R.S. provided a place on returns for a corporate seal was for the convenience of those corporations wanting to use their seal. The only actual filing requirement was a corporate officer's signature. A corporate seal wasn't really necessary at all!

14

How to Keep Embezzlers Out of the Till

Up! Up! Up! Ye men of Puritan Boston! Raise a blast of indignation that shall purify her streets, make it too hot for bad men to tarry; fire the press, the pulpit, and public opinion; kindle a flame that shall burn to the lowest hell; drive the plague spot from her face; sweep like a simoom the pestilence from our midst; start the thunderbolt of outraged justice; say that Boston, enslaved Boston, by the help of God, shall yet throw off the shackles of vice . . .

Rev. Henry Morgan,
"Boston Turned Inside Out!"

How ironic that my lowly talents as a bookkeeper could have made me wealthy by now—if only I had been born unscrupulous. With more nerve and less middle class morality I could still become well fixed. Here is how I would do it. See if you can figure out a way to stop me!

First, I find a job as the bookkeeper/office manager for some successful small contractor. Most people hate and despise bookwork, especially active types like contractors. Their prevailing attitude is, "I don't wanta have anything to do with the damn books. I turn all that crap over to my bookkeeper." When a good, competent bookkeeper is found, the average contractor is only too happy to turn over complete responsibility to him for all office details, including complete control over the accounting records. The only office function the contractor retains is signing checks and once in awhile looking in the accounts receivable ledger to see who owes him money. So, finding a job with broad accounting responsibilities is easy.

The first official act in my new position is to tidy things up a bit by getting the outside C.P.A. fired. C.P.A.'s really aren't much of a hazard to resident embezzlers. Small businessmen never pay their C.P.A.'s enough to ever have them do much in the way of auditing. A businessman's aversion to C.P.A. fees lies somewhere between paying taxes and traffic fines. Nevertheless, C.P.A.'s are an uncomfortable nuisance. They may accidently stumble onto something. Besides, they are easy to get rid of.

I sidle up to the boss and say, "Look, why pay that damn C.P.A. a fancy fee? He's not really doing anything for you. I can do everything he is doing and you're already paying me to be here full-time anyway." That, usually, is enough to get the C.P.A. out of the picture. Now that that is done, I have complete control of the books.

Next, I warm up by having the company take care of my incidental expenses. I start taking $20 to $30 a week out of the petty cash box. The Boss works the cash box over pretty good himself. It's filled with illegible receipts, I.O.U.'s, bits of string, cryptic notes, rubber bands, and chewing gum wrappers; so slipping in some phony petty cash receipt slips is easy. Besides, I'm the one responsible for keeping it replenished with cash and accounting for its disbursements.

Next, I order additional company credit cards. Since I open all of the mail, it is easy to intercept them. They are what I use for such things as my personal car expenses.

Using the company name, I start buying personal items from suppliers we do a large volume of business with. Materials for my new swimming pool, a few appliances, etc. I pull the invoices for these items from the support attached to the supplier's statements. Nobody ever checks supplier's statements for supporting documentation so the missing invoices are never noticed.

I also indulge in a little petty thievery, just for kicks. I take postage stamps, tools, and bars of soap from the washroom home at night in my brief case.

Now, I get down to serious business. I open up a separate company bank account in a strange bank some distance away—only to that bank I represent that I am the company's president and authorized check signer. Next, I rent a couple of post office boxes and I use them as addresses for some fictitious supplier's invoices that I have printed up. I also set up bank accounts for these phony companies in other banks. Now I am ready to work my employer over as he sits there, fat, dumb, and happy, relieved that a good detail man is running his office for him.

When things get busy and he is running around trying to manage several different jobs at once, I start typing up phony suppliers' invoices. I slip them in with the legitimate invoices left on his desk to be paid. It's not likely, but if he should happen to question one of them, I fire back with, "Oh, that's some stuff for the school job we worked on last month." The Boss is too busy to check out any explanation that sounds half-way reasonable to him so he lets it pass. I deposit the company's checks for these phony invoices in my phony bank accounts. Later, I extract the funds in cash.

Then I start overpaying legitimate suppliers. I hold the checks the Boss signs for payment of the month's invoices until the next month's statements arrive. I then have him pay the amounts shown owing on the statements, too. When the suppliers refund the duplicate payments, I deposit them in my phony company bank account. I also regularly overpay the company's business and payroll taxes and do the same with those refunds. This is easy to do because no one ever checks my calculations on the company's tax returns except the taxing agencies themselves.

Every once in awhile money comes in on an old account that had previously been written off as a bad debt. I take this money, too. There is no control over old accounts previously written off so nobody ever notices.

When the Boss gets frantically busy, I walk into his office and say, "Hey Harry, how about signing some checks for me? I have to pay the bills today."

"Dammit, I'm busy! How many do you need?" I pretend to figure for a few seconds, "Let's see, we got to pay the telephone bill, the lumber company, the plumber,... oh, I guess 15 will do it."

I actually need only 14. The fifteenth pre-signed blank check I make out to myself for a substantial amount of cash. I enter this check in the check register as having been for materials and supplies. When the bank statement comes the following month, I extract the cancelled check and destroy it. Since I'm the one who reconciles the bank account there is no problem doing this.

Every month customers mail in money to be applied to their accounts. I always keep several of their checks. I enter the amounts in the accounts receivable journal all right but I don't include them when I total the journal pages. I also enter their receipt on the respective customer ledger cards in the account receivable book. I then juggle the sales journal so as to make the accounts receivable control card balance. Since I have complete control over the mail, the bank deposits, the cash receipts journal, and the accounts receivable ledger, no sweat. My additions in the journals and ledgers are never checked, so I sleep soundly at night.

When a job superintendent phones in that a man on one of the jobs quits, I keep him on the payroll an extra week. Only I take the guy's check and fraudulently endorse it over to myself. Since I pass out the payroll checks for distribution to employees, it is easy to retain the phonies. There is normally a lot of turnover among construction workers. When you have 40 or 50 guys working at times on several jobs, it is impossible for the Boss to keep track of them all or to remember their names. Once in awhile, though, when the Boss is signing payroll checks he may hit me with, "Hey, I thought this guy quit?" I come over and look at the check, "Yeah, he quit the end of last week. He still had some time coming. He wants us to mail it to him." (We pay the following week for the previous week's work).

The boss signs the check. "Lazy so'nso's. They earn enough to buy a fifth of whiskey and then they quit on you."

I only sweat a little bit while this is going on. If he had pressed me on it, I would have taken it back from him and said I would check it out. Then I would get busy doing something else and tear it up later.

Now, I present my own salary check for the Boss's signature. It shows $750 gross, $200 withholding, and $550 net pay for the month. That is what I get paid all right so the Boss signs it. I enter it that way in the payroll journal too, but I change the page totals in the payroll journal. I increase gross wages by $1,000 (a debit) and I also increase income tax withheld by $1,000 (a credit). Everything balances and net wages still agree with cash disbursements. I'm the one who prepares the quarterly payroll tax returns so I report it that way to the government and have the company pay in the extra $1,000 withholding tax for me. At the end of the year, I prepare the employee's annual W-2's. When I come to my own, I increase gross wages by $12,000 (12 months at $1,000 per month) and I also increase the income tax withheld from my salary by the same amount. I file my income tax return with the W-2 attached and get a refund of about $9,000 from the I.R.S. (I don't get the full $12,000 back because including it in my gross income meant I had to pay taxes on it.)

I could take more money doing things but the Boss already worries a lot about why he doesn't seem to be making more money then he is. "Blasted unions keep upping their wages, blasted suppliers keep increasing their prices, and the blasted government keeps taking everything that is left over. It's getting to where a man can't make an honest living anymore."

I don't want the Boss to worry any more than he is. It would be a shame if something happened to him now.

You think the foregoing is farfetched, do you? Well, I have seen every one of these embezzlement techniques, or a variation thereof, perpetrated on someone at one time or another.

It is estimated that billions of dollars are lost every year to embezzlers. I believe it. Small businesses in particular are susceptible because they usually have lousy control over their assets and records. "Internal control" is the terminology used by accountants to describe the methods and procedures businesses use to prevent their assets from being stolen or misappropriated. There are two basic principles to good internal control:

1. Separation of duties between different employees.
2. Checking and verification of records.

You will notice that in my hypothetical construction company embezzlements I had complete control over the records, all the way from creation of basic source documents to the preparation of financial statements and tax reports. There was no separation of accounting duties between separate individuals. Also, no one ever checked my work—not even test-checked it. Naturally, my contractor employer got embezzled. He was asking for it. If I didn't do it, someone else would. There was no internal control. Yet the situation I described is common among small businesses.

Typically, a small business owner has had old Mabel or old Pete in the back room there doing the books for the past 15 or 20 years. He just knows that he or she is as honest as the day is long. He's probably right. Most people basically are pretty honest. But even honest people will steal if they are faced with a personal financial crisis. Particularly if they are reasonably sure they won't get caught. As a matter of fact, there are many people who will steal even without a financial crisis if they know they can get away with it.

So the basic rule is—don't provide people with the opportunity to steal. Divide the accounting duties up among several people so that it takes collusion to cover anything up Iave their work checked and reconciled. Suppose, in my example, that someone else had recorded receipts and made bank deposits? It wouldn't have been so easy for me to take money then, would it? Suppose all job invoices required the approval of a job superintendent or the Boss before payment? Suppose someone else did the bank reconciliation and prepared the tax reports? Suppose payroll checks had been accompanied by employee time cards which had been previously approved by the job foremen? Suppose the footings in journals and ledgers had been test-checked and my detail receivable cards balanced to the receivable control card? If these things had been done, it would have been hard for me to embezzle. Not impossible, but hard. That, however, is all that you are really after. A dedicated embezzler can eventually find a way to steal even under a tight internal control situation. But there are very few dedicated embezzlers around. Most embezzlers are opportunists. If they have to work hard in order to embezzle, they probably won't.

How can you have tight internal control when you are a small company? How can you segregate duties when there is only one office employee?

The answer is that the owner himself must step in and become part of the office and an unofficial auditor. A small business owner can exercise considerable internal control even if he is not a trained accountant. Doing nothing more than evidencing a keen interest in the books will scare away many potential embezzlers.

Here are some things a small business owner can do himself that will provide good internal control:

1. Open the mail.
2. List mail receipts before turning them over to the bookkeeper.
3. Subsequently trace his listing of mail receipts to the cash receipts journal.
4. Personally sign all checks, but only after they've been properly completed.
5. Personally approve and cancel all documentation in support of disbursements.
6. Review the bank reconciliation. Better yet, once in awhile do the bank reconciliation yourself.
7. Require that monthly statements be sent to all deliquent receivables and review them before they are sent out.
8. Personally approve all accounts receivable write-offs and discounts.
9. Periodically test-check accounts payable statements.
10. Personally do all the hiring.
11. Personally approve, sign, and distribute all payroll checks.
12. Become personally acquainted with all of the company's fixed assets.

13. Periodically supervise a physical inventory of stock and materials.

14. Require that all employees take periodic vacations and that employees who handle funds be bonded.

15. Require that cash sales be controlled by cash register tapes or locked counter receipt boxes which are reconciled to cash deposits.

16. Have an outside accountant come in periodically to review the books and make test-checks of the records.

I know from experience that you won't do all of these things but don't ever say I didn't warn you. By the way, you don't happen to need a good bookkeeper and office manager, do you?

15

How to Buy a Business Without Getting Had

"Opportunity," says Mr. Dooley, "knocks at iv'ry man's dure wanst. On some men's dures it hemmers till it breaks down th' dure an' then it goes in an' wakes him up if he's asleep, an' afterwards it worrucks f'r him as a nightwatchman. On some men's dures it knocks an' runs away, an' on th' dures in some men it knocks an' when they come out it hits them over th' head with an axe. But iv'ry man has an opportunity."

Finley Peter Dunne,
Mr. Dooley Says

Some people start out on their own by buying an already existing business. This has its advantages. In the first place, buying an existing business automatically eliminates a future competitor. Stepping into someone's shoes means there will be one less person to split up the local market with. Second, buying a business saves you time. It usually takes years of thrashing around to develop the facilities and contacts needed to establish a going business. Buying one that has been around for awhile gives you a running start. Third, if you stay on good terms with the former owner, you may be able to glean valuable tips and leads from him. People who sell out sometimes do so because they are just plain worn out and tired of the rat race. They may have accumulated excellent experience and insight. They may have well-formulated ideas as to how to expand and become more profitable. But they just can't take it anymore. There isn't enough energy and capital left to carry out their ideas. However, you, being fresh to the fray, can take the ball and run with it.

There are two big problems, though, with buying a going business. First of all, it's never easy to find a decent one that is for sale.

Most businesses being offered for sale are dogs. Too often it's a case of a guy trying to salvage something before he loses everything. But not always. Sometimes good businesses are sold for legitimate reasons. The owner may be wanting to retire or perhaps he has a health problem. Maybe he has become involved in something else that is more profitable. Possibly his business has become so profitable he feels he can bail out at a fat price and relax awhile. But even if a business is a dog, it still may be worth considering if you can figure out how to solve the previous owner's mistakes.

As to how to find a business, here are a few tips: Accountants and lawyers are usually the first to know when a businessman decides to sell out. Try sending a short letter to all of the accountants and lawyers in the area where you want to be located. Describe the kind and size of business you are looking for and roughly how much you expect to be able to pay. If your first circularization doesn't bring any response, follow up with another a few months later. Accountants and lawyers receive a horrendous amount of junk mail so sometimes it takes awhile to get their attention. Bankers are also good people to make your interest known to. Visit the local bankers in person. On something like this they can often be helpful. Trade association directors know a lot of gossip about their members, including who may be thinking of selling out. If the type of business you are looking for has a permanent director for its trade association look him up. The classified ad sections of major newspapers contain listings of businesses for sale. Classified ads are definitely a long-shot source, though. Most worthwhile businesses change hands via word of mouth. They don't need to be advertised.

Of course, you can always just go around and start knocking on doors. Look up all the businesses that seem to be about the size you think you can handle. Then simply walk up to their owners and ask point blank if they'd like to sell out. Wait until the end of the week before you do this though. A businessman's inclination to sell varies in direct proportion to how far along in the week he is. After a rotten Monday, Tuesday, and Wednesday, you may catch him in the right mood by Thursday or Friday.

The second problem, once you have found a business for sale, is figuring out what it is worth. What is a reasonable price? Take the Doozy Mfg. Co. for example.

As you will recall from an earlier chapter, Doozy earned $5,000 after an owner's salary of $15,000 and his business had a net worth value of $65,000. How much is Doozy Mfg. Co. worth? How much would *you* pay for the right to a $15,000 a year salary plus a $5,000 profit?

The small business world's eternal question: "How much should I pay for this company?" As a C.P.A., I am constantly asked either this or the converse, "How much should I sell out for?"

I have seen numerous businesses bought and sold. I have testified as an expert witness in court trials as to the value of businesses. I have read countless articles on small business valuation written by experts. I have fought the I.R.S. over the estate tax values of deceased taxpayers' businesses. So, I should be a good person to ask—How much is a business worth? *Answer*—I don't know! Furthermore, no one else knows either. Anyone who says he does is a liar. Either that or else he is naive.

No one can know because there *is* no answer. The original question, remember, was, "How much would *you* pay for this company?" "You" is the problem. Ask a thousand people the same question and you will get one thousand five hundred different answers. (The extra five hundred is because half of the people will subsequently change their minds.)

The average of thousands of answers is how the marketplace determines the price of things. But there is no marketplace for the purchase and sale of small businesses. There are only isolated buyers and isolated sellers. The prices at which small businesses change hands depend upon their individual quirks and prejudices and motives.

The value of a business, quite simply, is whatever someone else is willing to pay for it. This is easy to define but hard to determine. There is no Wall Street marketplace for the purchase and sale of small businesses. Furthermore, no two businesses are ever quite alike.

So how do you go about finding out how much an informed, rational buyer would be willing to pay for a particular business? What someone pays is usually pretty closely related to the amount of future profits he thinks the business can be reasonably expected to earn. In other words, what sort of return on his investment does he expect the business to give him?

As a practical matter, prices usually range somewhere between the value of the business' net worth (the minimum price) and ten times the average earnings (the maximum price).

Multiplying earnings by some factor is known as the "capitalization of earnings" method of valuing a business. It is the most logical of any so-called formula approach. The theory is this: If you put your money in a bank account, it will draw approximately 5% interest. Therefore, since 5% is the going rate of return for the use of your money, the price you pay for a business should be at least whatever it takes to make its earnings equal 5% of its purchase price.

In Doozy's case that would be:

$$\text{Price} \times 5\% = \$5,000 \text{ earnings}$$
$$\text{Price} = \frac{\$5,000}{5\%} = \$100,000$$

Pay $100,000 for the Doozy Mfg. Co.? No way! Putting your money in Doozy's business is not the same thing as putting it in the bank. Bank savings are safe, secure and can be withdrawn at any time. Investments in the likes of Doozy have substantial risks associated with them. It isn't hard at all to lose everything in a small business investment. Furthermore, Doozy's investment dollars are not liquid. Money put into Doozy will be tied up for a long period of time. Clearly a bank's capitalization rate of 20 times earnings is too high. (Note: $1/5\% = 20$.)

Capitalization rates for business investments must be scaled downward so as to take into account greater risk and less liquidity. Most small businesses change hands at prices ranging somewhere between 1 to 10 times earnings.

The Small Business Administration, in its publication, "Checklist for Purchasing a Business," recommends that no small business be valued at more than 4 to 5 times its annual earnings.

A good guide as to what particular rate to use is Dewing's Capitalization Rate Chart. Arthur Stone Dewing was a famous financial analyst and economics professor. In 1953, he listed seven capitalization categories in his book, *The Financial Policy of Corporations.* They are as follows:

(1) *10 times earnings*—Old established businesses with large capital assets and excellent goodwill. Very few companies fall into this category.

(2) *8 times earnings*—Old established businesses that are successful but that require considerable managerial care.

(3) *7 times earnings*—Strong, well-established businesses that are sensitive to the general economy; that are vulnerable to recessions. They require considerable managerial ability but little special knowledge on the part of executives.

(4) *5 times earnings*—Medium sized businesses that require comparatively small capital investment and only average executive ability. These businesses are highly competitive but established goodwill is of distinct importance.

(5) *4 times earnings*—Small, highly competitive businesses requiring small capital investment. These are businesses that practically anyone, even with little capital, may enter.

(6) *2 times earnings*—Businesses, large or small, which depend upon the special, often unusual skill of one or a small group of managers. They involve only a small amount of capital and are highly competitive with high mortality rates.

(7) *1 times earnings*—Personal service businesses. They require little or no capital. The manager must have special skills and thorough knowledge of his subjects. The earnings of this type of business depends upon the manager's skill rather than his "organization." He can sell the business, including its reputation and his "plan of business" but not himself, the only truly valuable part of his enterprise.

Dewing's Capitalization Ratio Chart, as you can see, is not a precise formula. It is a guide towards making an educated guess.

It is no different than picking the odds on a horse at the race track. There are many factors to consider:

How much competition is there? (How many horses are in this race and how well does he run in a crowd?)

What's the state of the economy and how will it affect the business? (Is the track slow and if so is he a good mudder?)

Are there any management or technically skilled people going along with the business? (How good are the jockey and trainer?)

How well established is the company? (What are his bloodlines?)

What is the company's financial condition? (Has he had any injuries lately and how much weight is he carrying?)

How has the earnings picture been? (How has he done the last few times out?)

As an example, here is how Doozy Mfg. Co. stacks up. Earnings, last year, were $5,000. But that was for just one year. It's hardly fair to judge earnings capacity on one year's performance. Doozy has ups and downs just like any other small business. The average of several years would be more indicative. The previous five years' earnings are usually considered a good base period for averaging purposes.

Doozy's past earnings have looked like this:

Last year	$ 5,000
Two years ago	7,000
Three years ago	4,000
Four years ago	10,000
Five years ago	14,000
	$40,000 ÷ 5 years = $8,000 average.

Now we see that both the five year average and last year's earnings are misleading. Doozy's $8,000 average is considerably more than last year's $5,000 profit, but, on the other hand, earnings the last few years have been trending downward. It would be even more fair not only to average earnings but to also weight them according to their closeness in time to the present. Here is how that is done:

		WEIGHTED
	EARNINGS	EARNINGS
Last year	$ 5,000 x 5 =	$25,000
Two years ago . .	7,000 x 4 =	$28,000
Three years ago .	4,000 x 3 =	12,000
Four years ago . .	10,000 x 2 =	20,000
Five years ago . .	14,000 x 1 =	14,000
	15	$99,000

$99,000 ÷ 15 = $ 6,600 Weighted Average

$6,600 is a better indication of Doozy's earnings because that figure takes into account their *trend.*

Now, what would you pay for $6,600 in earnings and $15,000 a year salary? That sort of depends upon how a $15,000 salary strikes you. If you are a $12,000 a year man, $15,000 looks like a handsome salary. On the other hand, if you are a $20,000 a year man, $15,000 looks skimpy. In the latter case, you would likely look upon Doozy as really earning only $1,600 a year because you would feel that the owner's salary should be adjusted upwards to $20,000. This illustrates the fact that adjustments must often be made to financial statements in order to determine what income figure to capitalize. The amount of salary business owners take out is a tremendous variable. The amount taken depends upon income tax considerations, the working capital position of the company, and the owner's own personal standard of living. What is reasonable, you yourself must decide.

In addition to salary variations, there are often other items in a company's income statements that might cause distortions. For example, a company may be using fast depreciation write-offs for tax purposes that are greater than real economic depreciation. The company may have written off repair items that should have been capitalized as assets. There may be unusual, one-shot income items such as condemnation proceeds on properties or damages collected from a lawsuit. There may be substantial, unrecognized bad debts among the receivables. There may be severe distortions in income caused by inaccurate accounting for inventories. The point is that you never accept a small business' financial statements as the gospel. They must be analyzed and the figures presented in them verified.

But let's keep it simple. Let's assume that $15,000 is a reasonable salary for Doozy and that there are no quirks or bugs in his accounting. Assuming that the figures as stated are reasonable, what capitalization rate do we use?

Doozy manufactures coat hangers. This is a business that does not require a great amount of managerial talent or technical skill. It requires some capital but not an enormous amount. Coat hanger manufacturers are not tremendously affected by variations in the economy, either local or national. Goodwill is not of much importance in the business. People who buy coat hangers are not too fussy about whom they buy them from. Coat hanger brand names do not become household words. There is quite a bit of competition in the field. Many people are capable of manufacturing coat hangers, and it is easy to increase production in response to demand.

Five years ago, Doozy made $14,000 but last year he only netted $5,000. After checking around, we find out that Doozy got a divorce and has been hitting the bottle pretty heavy the last few years. Several business acquaintances are of the opinion that he hasn't been spending too much time at his business the last few years. It appears that conscientious management could reverse Doozy's declining earnings trend. For this reason, it probably isn't necessary to discount Doozy's purchase price for any anticipated future drops in earnings. New management should be able to halt further declines.

With these factors in mind, I personally would value Doozy Mfg. Co. at 4 times earnings—Category 5 on Dewing's Chart. That would make it worth $26,400 (4 x $6,600). But hold on. Awhile back we said that the value of Doozy's net worth was $65,000. How can you only pay $26,400 for assets that, after payment of liabilities, are worth $65,000? You can't. Remember, I said a business' net worth would be its minimum tranfer price. That is what you would use in this case because it is higher than the capitalization of earnings' formula. Doozy, you see, rather than sell out for $26,400 could merely liquidate his business and theoretically walk away with $65,000. Presumably, you would have to pay him at least that much, in order to obtain his company.

The foregoing is an illustration of the sorts of things involved in determining what price to pay for a business. Other factors sometimes enter into it. For example, you probably would be willing to pay more for a business if the seller gave you generous terms because the lower the down payment, the greater the leverage you would have. Some businesses bring higher prices than what you would ordinarily think because of monopolistic conditions. Professional sports franchises, radio stations, and trucking companies are examples. Bargain purchases may be possible, if a business' owner is seriously ill or if the business is in the hands of an estate.

Businesses in some industries sell at prices based on formulas involving gross sales or number of customers. Fuel oil companies, for example, sell for prices based on total oil gallonage sold. Milk delivery businesses sell for so much per customer. The exact prices vary with different localities.

A business may have some outside investments that are not really connected with the business itself. It may own valuable land or stocks that are passive investments not used in the business. These sorts of things would have to be valued separate and apart from the business itself.

Random Thoughts and Comments

• As to the kind of business you buy, stick to one that you know something about. It's hard enough being on your own as it is but if on top of everything else you don't know much about the business you are buying into, you are courting disaster.

• If you insist upon getting involved in some unfamiliar line of business, then take the time to get familiar with it. Work as an apprentice for awhile. Every business has tricks of the trade to it. Managers of large companies can afford to hire technical brains to take care of all their nagging little details. But you, the small businessman, are going to have to wear a lot of different hats. You yourself must be familiar with all aspects of your business.

• It's always a good idea to have the former owner sign an agreement not to compete. That way he can't change his mind next year and go back into business again as a competitor.

• Stay clear of businesses that have only one or a few major customers. Nothing is so volatile as a small business dependent upon a few major customers. Their sales base can evaporate overnight.

• It's usually best to buy the assets and goodwill of a company rather than the corporation itself. That way you know what you've got. When you buy the whole corporate structure you inherit whatever skeletons may be lurking in its closet. Like latent tax deficiencies, lawsuits, or other claims that haven't jelled yet at the time of closing.

• One of the oldest sales pitches in the world among people selling out goes something like this, "Actually, I could have made a lot more money in this business than I have but I really haven't pushed it very hard. Of course, the books don't show it, but there is a lot of potential here. You could easily double sales next year if you . . . etc., etc." Nonsense! Don't pay a puffed up price for this malarky. You are buying what the owner actually has, not what he could have had. If you make the business more profitable than he, it will be because of what you personally add to the business. Why should you pay him for what you yourself contribute?

• For John's sake hire your own lawyer and accountant to represent you and help analyze the deal. Don't ever depend upon the other guy's professional advisors. They can only serve one master at a time. And don't just depend upon your own wits either. You'd better believe the bit about "He who represents himself has a fool as a client." There are lots of points in a Sales Agreement that only an attorney will know how to handle—the seller's warranties and indemnifications, default provisions, contract terms, escrow arrangements, non-competition agreements, etc. Analyzing and verifying the seller's financial statements should be left to the talents of a sharp, aggressive accountant.

• It has been my experience that most people wind up paying too much for the businesses that they buy. As previously pointed out, finding a decent one that is for sale isn't easy. Consequently, once a person finally does find one, he tends to overvalue it because of its scarcity. This is a mistake. Businesses are not like gems or antiques. They do not become more valuable simply because they are rare. Always remember—a businesses' value depends upon the rate of return it gives the owner, nothing more.

• Above all else, take your time. Beat the bushes and shake the trees but don't be in a hurry to pick up the first deal that falls to the ground. Buying a business will be one of the most important capital commitments of your life. Take the time to investigate everything thoroughly. Don't be pressured into making a quick decision for fear of missing an opportunity. Small businesses are like streetcars. If you miss one now you may have to wait awhile but, there will always be another coming along later.

16

The Franchise Siren

Diana and her darling crew shall pluck your fingers
   fine,
And lead you forth right pleasantly to sup the honey
   wine.
To sup the honey wine, my loves, and breathe the
   heavenly air,
And dance, as the young angels dance. Oh God that I
   were there!

Ancient Hymn to the Moon Goddess, Diana

Next, ladies and gentlemen, by popular demand and in response to the fervid desires of all those thousands everywhere wanting to be in business for themselves, let me present—The Franchise Siren! Listen to it now as it sings its sweet song of opportunity while sidling up to a franchise prospect:

"Ya say ya wanta go inta business fer yerself? Ya say ya wanta be yer own boss? Ya say yer tired of the same old rat-race? Tell ya what I'm gonna do fer ya, kid: I personally am going ta help ya get set up ina business of yer very own. I'll pick the product fer ya, I'll find the location fer ya, I'll see that a building is constructed fer ya, I'll order yer equipment fer ya, I'll set up

103

pro-ceedures and methods fer ya, I'll train ya, I'll advise ya, I'll advertize fer ya, I'll help ya find financing—all ya have to do is run the place and collect all the money! Just dig up some starting capital, mortgage yourself to the hilt, pay me a modest fee, gimme a small piece of the action, buy yer supplies from me, sign this here simple little contract agreein' to do things my way and yer finally in business fer yourself. Watta opportunity! Why I did this fer a guy in San Jose last year and yer oughta see all the money he's made already. A guy with yer ability oughta be able to retire in five years. Better sign quick, kid. I gotta lotta guys wantin' this same territory."

_____

Pardon me for letting my cynicism surface. I guess I've seen too many phony francise deals in my time. At first glance, franchise operations look like a sound concept. Some of them are. But let's get one thing straight—running a franchise operation is not the same thing as being in business for yourself. What you are really doing is buying yourself a job—sort of a branch managership. True, as a franchisee, you have a certain amount of autonomy. But your modes of operation are severely restricted by the franchisor's regulations.

Franchises usually work this way—the franchise company has a prominent name and symbol. The many fast food chains that have spread throughout the country are examples. The franchise company sells rights to a local franchisee for a fee. In addition, the franchisee has to pay a percentage of his income to the parent company. Often he has to buy certain key ingredients and packages from the parent company. In return, the franchisee has the right to operate using what is deemed to be a well-established trade name, and using supposedly trade tested marketing techniques. He also is supposed to receive training, management advice, pooled advertising, and help in financing the necessary equipment and facilities.

The beauty of this arrangement as far as the franchise company is concerned is that it can expand its operations enormously in short order with very little capital. The individual franchisees, in effect, provide the expansion capital. By not having to sell a lot of capital stock to the public, no dilution of ownership occurs. The franchise company's leverage is tremendous.

The beauty of it for the local franchise operator is that he, theoretically, is in business for himself. Yet he has the protective umbrella of a big parent company over him.

While franchising definitely is not the same thing as being in business for yourself, perhaps it may be thought of as sort of a compromise. However, be careful! The franchise concept has expanded enormously the last few years. Like all previous business fads, it has attracted swarms of con men, flim-flammers, and rip-off artists. So if you ever consider a franchise proposition, for heaven's sake, investigate it thoroughly. Here is a checklist of the sorts of questions you should ask yourself:

1. Has your lawyer studied the franchise contract in detail?

2. Does the franchise call upon you to do anything your lawyer considers illegal or questionable in your particular locality? (A divorce service franchisee recently got into trouble because his parent company forgot to tell him that advertising divorce services was illegal in his state.)

3. Have you had an accountant analyze the financial projections and prepare a budget? Have you checked comparative prices of supplies you must buy from the parent?

4. Does the franchise give you an exclusive territory for the length of the franchise?

5. Is the franchisor connected in any way with any other franchise company handling a similar product or service? If so, what is your protection against competition from the second firm?

6. Under what circumstances can you get out of the franchise contract and what will it cost you to do so?

7. How many years has the franchise company been in business and does it have certified financial statements? If so, how sound is the company financially?

8. Does the franchise company have certified figures for other franchisees? Have you personally checked with other franchisees?

9. Does the franchise company provide:

   a. Management training?
   b. Employee Training?

c. Public relations and advertising?

d. Capital?

e. Credit?

f. Merchandising ideas?

g. Help in finding a location?

h. Help in constructing the facility?

10. Are you ready to trade some of your independence for the security of the franchise?

11. Are you ready to spend the rest of your business life with the franchisor and his product?

12. What can the franchisor do for you that you cannot do for yourself!?

If this list seems too long to remember, then just remember three things:

1. Have an attorney look the deal over.

2. Have an accountant look the deal over.

3. You yourself check with at least three other people already owning the same franchise. Ask them if they are making as much money as the parent company estimated. Ask them how much help the parent company has provided. Ask them if the parent company has lived up to its agreements.

For data on specific franchise companies, you can write the U.S. Department of Commerce for its publication: "Franchise Company Data."

Good luck to ya, kid.

17

Humbuggery

> You gullible green-grass goats! Can't you get it
> through your heads that you're being swindled outa'
> your eye teeth right now—this minute? There's a
> burglar in the bedroom while you're fiddling in the
> parlor!*
>
> "The Music Man," Meredith Willson

If there is one single concept that I hope to get through your head, it is this: Nobody is ever going to walk into your life and make you rich.

Watch yourself whenever someone approaches saying that, for the price of a modest fee, he will furnish you secrets guaranteeing instant wealth. There is nothing magic about wealth. It usually comes about because of the existence of one of three circumstances (or a combination thereof):

1. Being in the right place at the right time. In other words, being lucky. Many real estate fortunes are made this way. Discovering oil on the back forty of the family farm is another example.

---

*Quoted from "The Music Man" by permission of Frank Music, NYC, the copyright holders.

2. Having some unusual sort of talent. The Barbra Streisands, Joe Namaths, Sammy Davis Jrs., Picassos, and Ernest Hemingways of this world have the secret. Just copy them and you've got it made.

3. Having quite a bit of money to start out with. In other words, it takes money to make money. Both Howard Hughes and J. Paul Getty, for example, inherited nice stakes to begin with. They were able to multiply these into enormous fortunes. But I wonder how far they would have gotten if they each had to start out broke with a young family to feed?

There are other ways you can accumulate fairly sizable amounts of money. But you have to be willing to pay the price. You have to be willing to do and endure certain things that might be distasteful. I am sure, for example, that many individuals could have accomplished what *Playboy's* founder, Hugh Hefner, has done. But those who could, haven't. Probably because during the 1950's when *Playboy* was created, they wouldn't have been able to endure the embarrassment of conflicting mores or the fear of making fools out of themselves.

Doctors in this country make an awful lot of money. Contrary to popular folk lore, you don't have to be a genius to be a doctor. All you need besides reasonable intelligence is the willingness to endure about ten years of poverty and hard work. Plus the capacity of not being bothered by blood and gore and needles. Me, I can't stand blood, I faint at the sight of needles and I don't like gore, unless it is medium well-done. Otherwise, I think I could have made the grade.

There have been some high-paying jobs available overseas the past few years. Construction work in Viet Nam comes to mind. Unfortunately in order to cash in, you would have had to be willing to forsake comfort, friends, home, and a certain amount of personal safety.

Not very long ago, there was a golden opportunity to make a real pile of dough producing pornographic movies. The capital required to get into the porno business was small, the profit margins staggering, and the market was rapidly expanding. But how many guys could have overcome the smirks they would have gotten at the old class reunion when they explained what business they were in?

Many high level politicians seem to accumulate considerable wealth over the years. The exact process by which they accomplish this is somewhat of a mystery since political salaries, as a rule, are modest. Nevertheless, they do it. But how many qualified people are there who can stand the hypocrisy and phoniness of politics?

So, if someone advertises that you, little old you, can become rich by simply following some sort of magic formula—take it with a grain of salt. Let's face it, kids. There aren't many secrets in this world. And those who have them usually aren't about to share them.

People wanting to go into business for themselves are very susceptible to get-rich-quick schemes. Combine the chance of being in business for yourself with the chance of making a lot of quick, easy money and you've got an irresistible sales pitch. It's irresistible even if you are already in business for yourself. Years of hard work and worries for modest rewards make the typical small businessman a ripe candidate for any the-grass-is-greener pitch. Get-rich-quick fever is an insidious disease. By rights, the law ought to allow its victims the option of voiding all signed documents by reason of temporary insanity.

Throughout this book I keep referring to "promoters." What do I mean by that term? A promoter is a person who tries to talk you into giving him your money with the view towards putting together a deal that, supposedly, is mutually beneficial. Promoters try to infect you with the belief that you, via them, are going to become independent, healthy, wealthy, and wise. The thing about promoters that you have to keep in mind is that their proposals may be good deals or they may be bad deals, but for damn sure, they will always be good deals for the promoters. This, quite naturally, makes a promoter's judgement at best biased, and at worst fraudulent.

One trick of the trade always used by promoters is putting forth the impression that they are successful and well-to-do. Success breeds success, is their motto. They drive Cadillacs, never Volkswagens. They wear flashy tailored clothes, never off-the-rack suits. They always pay for your lunch and leave big tips. They often sport diamond rings, gold watches and monogrammed shirts. Invariably, they are highly skilled name droppers.

Promoters usually suffer the occupational disease of habitually spending money faster than they can con it out of the suckers. Which is to say—they are usually broke. That is, right up until the time they close their deal with you. The way, then, to smoke out a phony promoter from a legitimate businessman is to ask him one simple question: *How much money are YOU going to put into this deal, buster?*

If the promoter actually puts in as much cash as you, then you've probably got yourself an honest deal. It may still be a bad deal, but at least it's an honest one. On the other hand, if the promoter's funds are tied up in "non-liquid investments," or, if he thinks his proposition so valuable that no investment on his part is necessary, then you'd better start looking at him through smoked glass.

Now don't get me wrong. I admire promoters. You have to admire anyone who can make people believe in fairy tales. The better promoters have an almost Jesus-like ability to move people. This takes real, honest-to-goodness talent. I, myself, have tried influencing people on occasion. Whatever it takes, I haven't got it. So I've resigned myself to never being able to earn as much as promoters. It's still fun, though, to stand back at a distance and watch them operate.

We should all be thankful that more promoters don't enter politics. This is a temptation because politics is a con game too. Promoters in private practice have distinct practical limitations as to how many people they can bilk. Put them in politics though, and they become a public menace. There they've got the chance to fool people on a really grand scale.

Every current business fad becomes a promoter's fair game. For many people, not being "in" on today's "in thing" is the worst of all possible fates. Promoters know this. So every time a new fad comes along (electronics, plastics, computer leasing, real estate trusts, recreational property, conglomerates, or what have you) it is sure to attract promoters like honey attracts bears.

Tax shelters, in particular, are a popular promoter vehicle these days. People interested in tax shelters are in high tax brackets and earn lots of money. This makes tax shelters doubly attractive. Not only are they a fad but they are a fad of the rich as well.

I remember a highly skilled promoter a few years ago who assembled a group of wealthy investors. He talked them into turning over large sums of money to him to invest on their behalf in tax shelters. Some of the investors' money actually was invested in a few real estate ventures, all of which turned out to be losers. However, the promoter used a big chunk of the investors' money to finance some of his own private promotional schemes. Another big chunk was used to pay the promoter management fees; to pay for his travel, entertainment, and office expenses; and to buy a few assets used personally by the promoter—such as an airplane, a boat, and a beach cabin.

His wealthy investors loved him. He produced such great tax losses for them. Once in awhile a few of them would get restless when they heard rumors as to what some of their money was actually being spent on. Whenever this happened, the promoter would call a partnership meeting. He knew that it was again time to talk to them and cast another spell. Just an hour or so of his obtuse, bombastic magic and they would all once again come back into the fold. It took about five years before the investors woke up to the fact that they had been had. By that time all their funds had been dissipated.

Franchise operations, as discussed earlier, are also a fertile field for promoters. Franchise deals are a natural because they can so often be put together with nothing but paper. Also, the concept has such strong appeal to those yearning to get into business for themselves.

Another popular promotional thing in the past has been multi-level distributorships, alias pyramid sales, alias chain sale distributorships. These are a business adaptation of the old chain letter gimmick. They work this way:

Assume that there is a product to sell. It can be anything —cosmetics, household supplies, books, etc. What the promoter does is charge you, say, $5,000 for the right to be a distributor of his products. As a distributor, you get a 30% commission on sales. In addition, you have the right to sell distributorships to others. If you sell a distributorship, you receive one-half of the new distributor's $5,000 distributorship fee plus a small percentage of his sales. To make it even more attractive, you also receive a percentage of whatever distributorships the second distributors sell. In this fashion, a pyramid of several levels is created with small pieces of the action filtering up to the guys at the top. As any fool can plainly see, all a person has to do in order to earn $50,000 to $100,000 a year is to go out and sell about 12 distributorships a year. Forget about selling the original product. Just sit back and collect your cut of whatever the guys you sold distributorships to sell.

I'm sure you can already see what the problem is. Pretty soon, everyone is running around like mad selling distributorships instead of the product. Which is fine, except that pretty soon you run out of people. Suppose that in year one a person sold twelve distributorships, that the next year each of the new distributors sold twelve distributorships, and so on.

Here is what you would get:

Year	Distributors
0	1
1	12
2	144
3	1,728
4	20,736
5	248,832
6	2,985,984
7	35,831,808
8	429,981,696
9	5,159,780,352
10	61,917,364,224

Within six years you have as many distributors as there are people in the City of Los Angeles. Within 7-½ years every man, woman, and child in the United States is a distributor. Less than a year later and you have taken in all of the people of Red China. Before nine years are up, every person in the world is a distributor. At the end of ten years you would have about five times as many distributors as there have been people who have ever lived on earth.

This illustrates, of course, the old chain letter fallacy. He who starts the chain makes out just great, but those coming aboard later on lose their dough to those at the top.

The vulnerability of people to being conned, duped, flim-flammed, fooled, cheated, tricked, had, gulled, and hoaxed never ceases to amaze me. Some years ago, I became briefly involved with a group of investors in a gold mining venture. Now, really, a *gold* mining venture? That's a bit Brooklyn Bridge-ish, isn't it? But these weren't farm boys. These were intelligent, well educated, and, in some cases, professional people.

I knew nothing, personally, about mining. But twenty minutes' research at the Public Library taught me that at that time, practically all of this country's gold was produced as a mere byproduct of other mineral production activities. At that time, nobody mined gold, per se. The reason was simple. Because of the Government's pegged price of gold, it cost more to mine and refine gold than the gold itself was worth. Of course, this wasn't the message the investors wanted to hear. They preferred to believe that their promoter friend had couped the world's leading engineering brains by developing a secret process that made it economical to mine gold.

I kept track of this venture for three years. Every winter it was the same thing.

The promoter would come down out of the North and talk his investors into contributing more funds. In the spring he would disappear back up in Alaska with the money, only to reappear the following winter looking for more.

Always he was just one step away from attaining success and instant wealth for all concerned. Always some last minute, unexpected problem developed. Early winter freezes, floods, delayed deliveries of supplies, equipment breakdowns, or what have you. The only actual equipment breakdown, as far as I'm concerned, was in the investors' heads.

In the final analysis, there are just two wealth building secrets, if you want to call them that. The first one is: You have to be willing to take a chance. Like the proverbial turtle, you will never get anywhere unless you are willing to stick your neck out. When it's fourth and one, you have to go for a touchdown instead of dropping back ten yards to punt. Wealth is a direct function of the so-called risk-reward ratio. The greater the risk, the greater the *potential* reward.

The second "secret" is: Use your imagination—let it soar. Elvis Presley once said, "If you're gonna get any place these days, you gotta be different." Very true.

In my home town, for example, there is one very successful automobile dealer whose trademark it is to appear on TV ads dressed in silly costumes with a sledgehammer, which he proceeds to use to bash in the fenders of one of his cars. He, at the same time, laughs insanely, giggles, says inane things, and in general makes a complete ass of himself. He also sells cars like crazy.

On a less dramatic scale, being successful by being different usually involves thinking up some sort of low cost process, product, service, or method that isn't now being done. Whatever it is, it must be unique enough to have an untapped market. By the time you hear of an already existing idea, it's usually too late. Imitating others merely sets you up for a head knocking contest with an established competitor plus all the other guys who decided to jump onto the bandwagon too. Copycats usually don't prosper.

What it boils down to is this: You can start a conventional business, plod along, and work hard. Chances are you won't get rich but, on the other hand, you probably won't starve to death either. With a little luck you may wind up with a very comfortable living.

Or else, you can shoot the works and try to get rich quick. You can dream and scheme, wheel and deal, promote and risk all. You may make it big or you may fail. The chances are overwhelmingly in favor of the latter. But at least you will have had your chance. For some people, this is all they ask. For them it is better to have tried and lost than never to have tried at all.

I know my message is a lonely voice in the wilderness. The shouts and roars of the Dare-to-be-Great crowd are overpowering. Positive and optimistic messages always drive out words of caution. People do *so* want to believe. Consequently, we pessimists usually play to empty houses. Fortunately, we do have one small satisfaction. In the end we are traditionally permitted to say, "I *told* you so."

18

Two, Four, Six, Eight; Let's All Incorporate

Corporation—*Kawr poh RAY shun*—a body created by law which can act as a person in legal matters. It can hold property, make contracts, and file suits. A corporation is subject to most of the same penalties as a person. It can be fined, sued, or even put out of existence by law, but it can not be put in prison. The corporation may owe money, but the debts are obligations of the company, not of the individual stockholders.

The World Book Encyclopedia

One of the questions people going into business for themselves always ask is whether or not they should incorporate. There are both advantages and disadvantages. Overall, though, I think corporations are the best form of organization.

First of all, there is limited liability. You can't be sued for your corporation's debts, except for Federal withholding taxes and those debts that you personally guaranteed. From a practical standpoint, this isn't all that big of an advantage because often you'll be called upon to cosign your corporation's obligations. Certainly the bank will require personal guarantees on its loans. In addition, a corporation does not protect you from torts that you are personally involved in. ("Torts" is a term that the law uses for damages from accidents, improper work, and intentional wrongs such as slander or assault and battery. You should carry broad insurance coverage for torts.) Still, despite these limitations, if disaster strikes, you are usually able to walk away with a greater portion of your skin if you have a corporate shell to hide behind.

In addition, there can be tax advantages from being incorporated. I'll cover these in more detail when I discuss Tax Shelters. Briefly, though, it is possible to save taxes because of certain fringe benefits available to corporate employees; because of the superiority of corporate retirement plans versus self-employed retirement plans; and because corporations can have fiscal tax years ending in months other than December.

There is one other tax advantage to being incorporated that I can't document. It is based purely on my own personal opinion. I don't think you stand as much a chance of being audited by the I.R.S. when you are incorporated. As you undoubtedly know, the I.R.S. is completely computerized. Income tax returns are analyzed by computers for statistical variations that indicate a high probability of deficiencies. When you operate your business as a sole proprietorship, you have to deduct many items on your return that aren't "normal" for most individual taxpayers. Therefore, according to my theory, there is a greater chance of the computer finding something on your return it doesn't like the looks of—whereupon, it will spit out your return for review by an agent. On the other hand, if you report as a corporation, the things you deduct will seem "normal" when compared to other corporate tax returns.

There are a few other potential corporate tax advantages that are somewhat exotic in nature. It is possible to sell your corporation tax free by exchanging its stock for stock of another corporation. And, you can merge or combine your corporation with another corporation tax free.

It is easier to transfer or split up ownership of a business when it is in the form of shares of capital stock. For example, you can conveniently make periodic gifts of shares of stock to your kids. If you want to sell a partial interest in your business, it is more easily done with shares of stock.

There are some disadvantages to being incorporated. The main one is that, under the wrong set of circumstances, a corporate structure can turn into a tax trap.

For example, suppose you are drawing a salary for living expenses from your corporation but the corporation itself is having tax losses. Then you are in the position of having to pay income tax on your salary even though the business itself is losing money.

Corporations are subject to double taxation. That is, corporations pay tax on their income and then their stockholders pay tax on this same income again if they take out dividends, or if they sell their stock, or if the corporation is liquidated. Of course, you can get around this by taking profits out as salaries instead of dividends. Salaries are deductible. Therefore, they reduce the corporation's taxable income. However, salaries must be reasonable in amount in relation to the services performed. Otherwise the I.R.S. can disallow them.

Suppose your corporation gets a whale of a good purchase offer on its plant and real estate. So you go ahead and sell the plant and relocate the business. Now, suppose that you would like to use part of the sales proceeds for personal purposes. Like taking a trip around the world or paying off your house mortgage. If you take any of the proceeds out of your corporation for these purposes, you will have to pay tax on them even though the corporation itself was taxed on the original sale.

Small corporations can usually get around these types of problems by making a special tax election. It is called the "Subchapter S" election. Subchapter S was enacted to give small businesses the opportunity of having the legal advantages of a corporation but the tax advantages of a partnership or individual proprietorship. When this election is made, the corporation itself pays no income tax. Instead its income or loss is reported on the stockholders' returns just as though it were a partnership. Subchapter S stockholders can draw money out of their corporation without double taxation and they can deduct any losses the corporation may have on their own personal returns. Unfortunately, Subchapter S is not as simple as I describe it. It is loaded with special rules and it contains some tax traps of its own for the unwary. You will have to have professional help in order to safely use it. Nevertheless, properly used, a Subchapter S election can solve a lot of the tax problems small corporations might otherwise have.

Corporations are separate legal entities, so there is more paperwork and formality involved with them. You have to have board of directors' meetings, annual stockholders' meetings, corporate resolutions, and minutes and all that. Transactions between you and the corporation have to be supported by formal documents. Officers' salaries and bonuses must be authorized; corporate loans and advances to stockholders must be backed up by promissory notes and the proper bookkeeping entries; rental agreements between you and the corporation must be evidenced by written leases; etc. In other words, you have to respect your corporation's legal status as a separate entity. If you don't, then the I.R.S. can disregard some of the things you do and can trap you on some things you don't do.

In summary, I would say this: If you are making a lot of money, like $30,000 or more a year, you probably should be incorporated because of the potential tax advantages available to you.

If you are losing money or have a shaky operation, you probably should be incorporated because of the limited liability feature.

If you are somewhere in between, it isn't all that clear cut, but incorporation probably has more advantages for you than disadvantages.

If you don't incorporate, then you'll operate as a "sole proprietorship" if by yourself. If you have partners you'll be a partnership. Partnerships are not separate legal entities. They are only accounting entities. As a partner, you are responsible for *all* of the partnership's debts, not just your pro-rata share of them. Partnerships don't pay income taxes. The individual partners report their share of the partnership's income on their own individual returns. Partnership agreements can be either written or verbal.

If you are going into partnership with somebody, for Gawd's sake have a written buy-sell agreement drafted up between partners. As a matter of fact, you should have a buy-sell agreement in a corporation too if there are other stockholders. A buy-sell agreement can eliminate lots of future bickering and lawsuits. Without it, you have a problem whenever partners leave or die.

Without a prior agreement, how do you determine the value of the withdrawing partner's interest and how do you decide the terms by which he is to be paid? And having to deal with a deceased partner's widow without a prior agreement can be a very unfortunate experience—take my word for it.

Two-man partnerships and two-man corporations? Don't! I don't care how compatible you are to begin with, eventually there will be differences of opinion. When you're 50-50, there is no way to reach a consensus. One or the other of you may, for a time, give in to the other's decisions. But this just leads to brooding. Eventually the passive partner will pay homage to human nature and explode. All of his prior grievances will spill forth, neatly packaged and inventoried. If he doesn't explode, then he'll just find some other way to get back at you. As one very experienced partner once told me, "There are a lot of different ways to fight." The passive partner will find some sneaky way in which to be an obstruction. In small businesses, this is easy to do.

When two guys first go into business together, everything is love and kisses. They boost one another's morale and reinforce each other's excitement. Then they have their first argument. From then on, it's all downhill. Usually they wind up fightin' and clawin' each other like two tomcats in a gunny sack.

If you're bound and determined to be in equal partnership with somebody, then you'd better have yourselves an ironclad, detailed agreement as to what happens when unresolvable disputes arise. Just remember that going into partnership with someone is like getting married and that now-a-days nearly one-third of all marriages end up in divorce.

19

How Much Capital
Do You Really Need?

Happiness is having ten cents . . . in front of a pay
toilet.

Rochelle Davis,
Happiness Is a Rat Fink

Every once in awhile, some guy walks into my office who is
contemplating going into business for himself and he has it all
figured out. He's lined up enough money to buy a little equipment, some supplies, and a few weeks' payroll. He has carefully
calculated that his first month's sales will generate enough money
to pay for his second month's operating expenses. Then his second
month's sales will pay for his third month's expenses, his third
month's sales will pay for his fourth month's expenses, etc., etc.
He figures he can keep going like that, living from month-to-
month, while his profits gradually build up his working capital.

Friends, it just doesn't work that way! There is a time lag
between the point when you buy labor and materials and the
point when they are converted into products. There is a time lag
between the point when they are sold. There is a time lag between

the point when the products are sold and the point when you collect the money.

In other words, there is a significant time interval between the point when you spend money and the point when it comes back to you again in the form of cold, hard cash. This is known as a company's business cycle. Business cycles usually last several months at least, although they vary quite a bit from business to business. Because of business cycles, the capital that you need is not just confined to supplies and equipment. You also have to invest in accounts receivable, inventory, prepaid expenses, and enough cash to pay current operating expenses. As far as your business is concerned, these items are permanent fixed assets too, just as much as your buildings and equipment.

To illustrate this, here is how that guy who came into my office figure out his cash budget for, say, the first two months of his operations:

CASH BUDGET
First Two Months' Operations

Cash Receipts—

Capital invested by owner	$ 5,000
Bank loan	5,000
Equipment loan	10,000
Sales proceeds	10,000
	$30,000

Cash Disbursements—

Cost of equipment	($15,000)
Cost of supplies	(500)
Cost of labor and materials	(7,000)
Cost of two months' overhead	(2,000)
Equipment loan payment	(500)
	($25,000)

Cash Surplus—	$ 5,000

Not bad. According to this, there should be $5,000 on hand at the end of two months. Enough to pay off the bank loan.

Nice try, but here is how it really works out:

	First Month	Second Month
Beginning Cash	$ –0–	$ 500
Cash Receipts–		
Capital invested by owner	5,000	–
Bank loan	5,000	–
Equipment loan	10,000	–
Sales proceeds	1,000	5,000
	$21,000	$ 5,500
Cash Disbursements–		
Cost of equipment	($15,000)	($ 500)
Cost of supplies	(500)	(500)
Cost of labor and materials	(3,000)	(6,000)
Cost of overhead	(1,000)	(1,000)
Utility deposits	(500)	–
Rent deposit	(500)	–
Freight and installation costs on equipment	–	(500)
Equipment loan payment		(500)
Legal, tax registration, and licensing fees	–	(500)
	($20,500)	($ 9,500)
Ending Cash–	$ 500	($ 4,000) o.d.

Zounds! Alchemy in the raw. $5,000 of cash surplus trans-mutes into a $4,000 bank overdraft–just like that! Zippo, presto. That's accounting magic for you. But wait! There is more to come. Would you believe that he has a $3,000 *profit* despite the $4,000 cash shortage? Watch:

Two Months' Income Statement

Sales	$16,000
Materials	(6,000)
Labor	(4,000)
Supplies	(1,000)
Overhead	(2,000)
Net Profit	$ 3,000

To prove that a $3,000 profit does, indeed, coexist with a $4,000 cash deficit, here is the balance sheet:

Balance Sheet at the
End of Two Months

Assets

Cash (overdraft—see below)	$ –0–
Accounts receivable	10,000
Inventory	2,500
Deposits and prepaid expenses	1,000
Equipment	15,500
Organization expense	500
Total Assets	$29,500

Liabilities

Bank overdraft	$ 4,000
Accounts payable	3,000
Bank note	5,000
Equipment contract	9,500
Total Liabilities	$21,500

Net Worth

Capital invested by owner	5,000
Net profit	3,000
Total Liabilities and Net Worth	$29,500

The owner runs out of money even though his business starts out profitable. The problem, of course, is that the owner only raised $20,000 of capital ($5,000 of his own money and $15,000 borrowed), whereas a minimum of $24,000 was needed. Still, $20,000 is a lot of money. I wonder what happened to it all? What happened–? Ahah! Come out of the phone booth Mr. Funds Statement, this is a job for you:

Funds Statement
First Two Months' Operations

Sources of Working Capital:

Owner's investment	$ 5,000
Bank loan	5,000
Equipment loan	10,000
First two months' profit	3,000
	$23,000

Uses of Working Capital:

Purchase of equipment	$15,500
Deposits and organization expense	1,500
Equipment loan payments	500
Investment in current working capi- tal (below)	5,500
	$23,000

Analysis of Working Capital:

Current Assets

Cash	($ 4,000)
Accounts receivable	10,000
Inventory	2,500
	$ 8,500

Current Liabilities

Accounts payable	$ 3,000

Current Working Capital	$ 5,500

People starting out in business for themselves invariably underestimate the time lag involved in their business cycle. They forget all about having to invest in accounts receivable and inventories. They also have a strong tendency to overestimate their beginning sales and to underestimate their beginning expenses. "Everything cost more than we thought it would!"—the universal lament of nouveau businessmen. It's easy to be optimistic when starting out. As a matter of fact, some optimism is necessary or else you probably won't even take the first step. Unfortunately, this causes entrepreneurs to nearly always wind up needing more working capital than what they had originally counted on. I would say, as a rough rule of thumb, that you had better add 50% to whatever capital you initially decide is necessary.

Don't count on profits to solve your working capital problems either. Paradoxically, early profits can increase a cash problem, as my example just showed you. When a business is profitable, it usually starts expanding and taking on more sales. Expanding sales make it necessary to invest in even more inventory, accounts receivable, overhead, and equipment. If a business expands too rapidly, it can have just as bad a cash problem as one that is losing money.

Of course, being profitable and short of cash is a much better situation to be in than losing money and being short of cash. It's much easier to borrow money to make up for a shortage when you are profitable. Furthermore, if you are profitable long enough, you eventually should start to catch back up. But that doesn't make it any easier while you are going through it.

Budgeting and estimating cash flows are not exact sciences. I don't care how smart you are or how realistic you try to be, the future always holds surprises. But knowing ahead of time that you will likely have problems should cause you to be sharper. Running scared is a much more desirable frame of mind to start out with than overconfidence.

20

Personal Living Expenses

Michelangelo had been taught by his father that labor was beneath a noble burgher; but it was the son's observation that Lodovico worked harder in figuring out ways not to spend money than he would have had to work in earning it.*

Irving Stone,
The Agony and the Ecstasy

Business and financial consultants tell you to keep personal living expenses low when starting out in a new business. Live frugally, they say, and plow the savings back into your business. Horse pucky! You should do just the opposite. Live high on the hog. Accumulate car and country club payments. Go on expensive trips. Live in a big house and keep a girlfriend on the side. Take big draws out of your business to cover it all.

Soon your business will come under severe financial pressure. Beginning capital is limited to what you can scrape up personally

---

*Quoted from Irving Stone, *The Agony and the Ecstasy*, © Doubleday and Company.

and what you can wheedle out of the bank. When this money is depleted by high living expenses, your fledgling business will quickly run short of working capital. Contrary to traditional advice, however, this is a desirable situation! There is nothing quite so stimulating as a big pile of bills and no money in the bank. Once the desperateness of such a situation sinks in, you will, in your terror, rise to heights never before dreamed of. You will have unwittingly unleashed the reservoirs of incentive and adrenalin heretofore lying dormant within yourself. These are the strongest assets any man can ever have. True, you run the risk of disaster and bandruptcy using this approach to summon them, but think how effective you will be after they arrive.

Any man who has been chased by the hounds of hell, and survived, turns into a very sound businessman. Prior calamities have molded some of the most capable small businessmen I know. For one thing, such a man turns out to be extremely cost conscious in the future. I mean, nobody sells him any ganip-ganops or frills. He sticks to basic necessities—period. He who has survived a near bankruptcy turns into a hard head. It isn't easy to fool such a man—he has heard it all before. He becomes a cynic and a pessimist, which makes for a more realistic outlook on business affairs. Finally, after a few narrow escapes, a man invariably comes to appreciate the smaller things in life. A few close calls beget perspective. He becomes content with his lot in life for he knows that, but for the grace of God and a little bit of luck, he could be a lot worse off than he is now.

It is of such things that happiness is made—plus successful small business management.

21

O. P. M.

Effort multiplied by the length of the effort arm
equals the load multiplied by the length of the load
arm.

The Law of Equilibrium

If you buy a piece of real estate for $10,000 and sell it two years later for $15,000, what is your rate of return?

Answer: ($5,000 profit ÷ $10,000) ÷ 2 years = 25%

Now, suppose you acquire the same piece of property for the same price only this time instead of cash you pay $2,000 down and sign a 6-1/4% promissory note for the $8,000 balance. Suppose you again sell the property two years later for $15,000. Is your rate of return again 25%? No! It is four times as great!

[($5,000 profit − $1,000 interest on note) ÷ $2,000] ÷ 2 years = 100%

There, you have just now been initiated into the secret O.P.M. Club. O.P.M. = Other Peoples' Money; also commonly known as "leverage." O.P.M. is the stock in trade of all big time promoters, regardless of their field. The principle is to use other peoples' money to finance investments because, by so doing, you multiply the profits made on your own cash investment. This is so because, regardless of how little you yourself invest, you still own 100% of all profits.

By spreading your own funds out as down payments in numerous projects, you can control a big pyramid of assets plus own all of the profits emanating from them.

An additional bonus is that you are, at the same time, taking advantage of inflation. Your loans will be repaid in the future with less valuable dollars. At current inflation rates, loan repayment dollars will have eroded by at least 9 percent per year by the time you actually get around to paying them back.

On top of this, the interest you pay is tax deductible. This means that Uncle Sam subsidizes your interest expense to the extent of whatever tax bracket you are in.*

Sounds like a hell of a way to make money, doesn't it? It is—which is why so many sharpies utilize leverage in their dealings. You too can use the very same principle in your own business. By using borrowed money, you can multiply the rate of return your own capital investment makes.

Of course, there is one thing you do have to be careful of. Leverage multiplies in reverse if the project backfires. If you own $10,000 completely pays for an investment opportunity, then all you have to lose is $10,000. However, suppose you leverage by borrowing an additional $90,000 to make a $100,000 investment. Now, if the investment goes sour, you not only lose $10,000 you also have to cough up another $90,000 plus accumulated interest besides.

Furthermore, if the word gets out that you are having problems, the creditors in your other ventures may get nervous and decide to call their loans also. The Domino Theory is a fact of life in the world of O.P.M. This is why every time recession shakes the economic tree, the air suddenly becomes filled with overfinanced promoters falling off the limbs they are on.

Nevertheless, leverage within reason makes sense. The reason I discuss it here is because many people have hang-ups over borrowing money, particularly children of the Depression. There are actually businessmen walking around who could borrow money but won't. Better that their businesses suffer from under-financing than borrow on their life insurance, or remortgage their

---

*Starting in 1972, Internal Revenue Service Code Section 163 (d) limited the amount of interest a non-corporate taxpayer can deduct when the loan is for investment purposes.

homes, or factor their receivables at the bank. Borrowing for them is an evil practice.

"The heck with paying the bank 10% interest," they say, "I'll just use my trade credit." Fine, but trade credit can be more expensive than bank interest. Many suppliers discount for prompt payment. Common terms are a 2% discount if paid within ten days of invoice, otherwise due within 30 days. That 2% might not look like much but it actually is an effective rate of 36% over the 20 days from the end of the discount period (the tenth day) and the 30th day when the invoice is due. Furthermore, many suppliers charge an extra 1% per month when you go past the 30 days. That amounts to 12% yearly interest. Yet, the small businessman who borrows to make his discounts is a rare bird.

Have enough self-confidence to be willing to utilize O.P.M. Believe me, no one is going to loan you money unless they have strong reason to feel that either you or the underlying security will repay them. Your faith in yourself should be at least equal to that of your creditors—otherwise you have no business being in business.

22

How High the
Money Tree?

Anti-monopoly in the United States ... has been
traditionally and, we think, necessarily ineffective.
Why? Primarily because it is possible for a corporation which has already grown to [large] size ... to
continue to acquire funds for further growth and
intensification of its monopolistic position. In fact, as
we have seen, under the ineffective anti-monopoly
legislation ... such monopolistic corporations are
uniquely able to obtain capital for further expansion
and further destruction of competition.[*]

Louis O. Kelso and Mortimer J. Adler,
The New Capitalists

Suppose a group of strangers walked up to you one day and
said, "Here's a million dollars. Take it. Use it in your business in
any way you see fit—no strings attached. We are loaning you this
money but there is no need to ever pay us back. Furthermore, we
will leave it up to you as to whether or not you pay us any
interest."

---

[*]Quoted from *The New Capitalists,* by Louis O. Kelso and Mortimer
J. Adler. Used with permission.

A far out dream? No. This, in effect, is what happens every time a large corporation floats a public stock issue. From a practical standpoint, money received from capital stock is like having a permanent loan. It never has to be repaid. The only cost a large corporation has on its outstanding stock is whatever dividends it distributes. However, there is no requirement that any actually be paid. Usually dividends are kept at a low rate. Or else they are paid out as additional stock rather than cash. Stockholders of large publicly held corporations expect to make money from appreciation of their stock's value rather than from dividends.

Access to stock equity money is one more big advantage large corporations have over the small. Who would ever think of buying stock in the corner garage or the local laundry?

Large corporations have several other sources of funds that are not accessible to small corporations. In addition to capital stock, large corporations can issue debenture bonds. Unlike stocks, bonds do eventually have to be repaid and interest does have to be paid on them. They are usually long-term, however. Ten year repayment schedules are common. Unlike most other loans, bonds are unsecured. Corporations don't have to tie up any of their assets as collateral for bond issues. Bond money isn't available to small corporations. Who in his right mind would think of loaning long-term, unsecured money to a small, closely-held corporation?

I'm sure by now everyone has heard of the "prime rate." This is the interest rate banks charge their very best customers, meaning large, giant corporations. Prime rates are usually significantly lower than the interest rates charged smaller clients—sometimes two or three points lower. This differential is accepted as being inevitable by most people but somehow it doesn't seem quite fair. There is a law on the books, you know, that prohibits businesses from discriminating between different customers as to the prices charged for their products. It is known as the Robinson-Patman Act and it applies to most merchandise. It doesn't apply, however, to the loaning of money. Consequently, banks can discriminate between borrowers to their hearts' content. They can charge General Motors 6-1/2% and you 9-1/2%. You really can't criticize them for this. Undoubtedly, you would do the same thing if in their shoes. Unfortunately, this state of affairs results in the highest interest rates being paid by the very people who can least afford to pay them—you, I, and all the other little guys.

Ever wonder what happens to all the premiums you pay on your life insurance policies? Most of this money is held in reserve for future losses and claims. Insurance companies earn income on these reserves by loaning much of them out to other businesses, usually for terms of from 10 to 15 years.

Guess who has access to this vast source of capital? It isn't the Ajax Roofing Company of Chickamauga, Georgia. It isn't the Squeehawkin Novelty and Variety Store either.

Another advantage enjoyed by large corporations is that they don't have to deal with banks. Instead of borrowing from banks like you and me and other mortals, they can borrow direct by issuing what is know as "commercial paper." Commercial paper is terminology for short-term, unsecured, corporate promissory notes. These pieces of paper are sold by large corporations in the open capital markets in large denominations of $25,000 or more. Interest paid on commercial paper is usually even lower than a bank's prime rate. Large corporations make extensive use of commercial paper borrowing. Not only is the interest cost low, but they avoid the fuss and muss of dealing with a bank besides.

By now, it should be obvious that the money tree's juiciest fruit is too high for most small businesses to reach. But there is no sense pining over it. Small business must accept reality and find other sources of capital. Well, then, what sources are there for the little guy?

The primary source, of course, is the small business enterpreneur himself. Accordingly, you should accumulate as much money ahead of time as you can before going into business on your own because that very probably will be the extent of any long-term capital you ever acquire. The only other common source of long-term capital is from the small business retaining its own profits. Unfortunately, profits can take a long time to build up, so expansion from this source can be mighty slow sometimes.

One way of maximizing beginning capital is to remortgage your house. If you own your own home, perhaps your equity has built up to the point where you can either get a second mortgage on it or else borrow back up on the first mortgage.

Small business does have one money source of its own that isn't available to large companies. That is the Small Business

Administration. Congress created the S.B.A. in 1953 with the specific objective of helping small businesses grow and compete. One way it helps is by loaning money. The S.B.A. will either guarantee a bank loan, participate with a bank in making a loan, or make a direct loan itself. Terms are for from five to ten years usually.

I'll describe S.B.A. activities in more detail in another chapter. Suffice to say now that they are chronically short of funds to lend and much of their efforts currently go towards making loans to disadvantaged businessmen. All other applicants are very carefully reviewed and a good many of them are turned down. The S.B.A. requires strong collateral for its loans. They also require that your personal investments be liquidated and the proceeds transferred into your business.

The S.B.A. has a reputation for putting loan applicants through a lot of red tape. In addition, borrowers must agree to certain restrictions as to the operation of their business including limits as to the amount of salary they can take out. Generally speaking though, the S.B.A. is reasonable in most respects and its personnel seem genuinely interested in being of help. I feel that it is definitely worthwhile to talk to them, especially if you are a member of a disadvantaged or minority group.

Local Development Companies (L.D.C.'s) are S.B.A. sponsored locally owned companies. Their purpose is to bring new industry into communities by developing such things as shopping centers and industrial parks. L.C.D.'s lease or sell the new facilities to small business once they are completed. The S.B.A. banks loan up to 90% of the project's costs. L.D.C. owners put up the rest. Because of restrictions on profits and low interest rates, lease-purchase terms can be very favorable for the small business participants.

Small Business Investment Companies are another semi-governmental source of money. S.B.I.C.'s are investment companies that are supposed to provide equity funds and development loans for small, and therefore by definition, risky businesses. S.B.I.C.'s are licensed by, and operated under, Federal regulations. Half to two-thirds of their money comes from governmental sources but they are owned by private investors and are run as profit making ventures. They were created by Congress in 1958 and originally they seemed like a good idea. A source of risk capital for small business is certainly needed. The encounters my clients have had with them, however, have not been satisfactory. S.B.I.C. money has proved to be very costly.

Here is a deal one of my clients made several years ago with a Small Business Investment Company:

My client needed $160,000 for expansion of his physical facilities. He applied for a loan from a local S.B.I.C. The S.B.I.C. loaned him the money, all right, taking a mortgage on his real estate and the newly constructed facilities as security. However, the loan was for only 5 years. At the end of that time it had to be either renegotiated or refinanced through conventional mortgage sources. Besides normal interest charges, the S.B.I.C. billed my client several thousand dollars to cover its loan processing costs. In addition, they were given an option allowing them to buy 20% of my client's capital stock at its current book value, exercisable within eight years. In addition, they had my client grant them another option allowing them to sell this same stock back to my client at its then book value.

Do you see what they did? They fixed it so that they had the best of both worlds. If things went bad, they were secured creditors because of the mortgage. If things went middling well, they could keep the mortgage and in addition, with the stock buy-back option, take 20% of my client's profits over the next eight years. If things went fabulously well, they could stay on as both stockholders and creditors. That particular loan cost my client a lot of money before he finally got them out of the picture. Of course, as the old saying goes, "Fifty percent of something is better than ninety percent of nothing." If you can't get money anywhere else, then S.B.I.C.'s are worth taking a look at. But they definitely should be thought of as a last resort.

Commercial banks are usually a small business' primary source of outside capital. The trouble with bank money, though, is that it is mostly short term borrowing and usually you have to sign your life away to get it. Banks seem to want about 200% security on loans of any consequence. In many respects, banks are difficult to deal with. Unfortunately, small businesses can't live without them. There are a lot of different arrangements available with banks. (See the next chapter for details.)

Other sources of money:

Friends—I don't advise borrowing from friends unless you don't care whether or not they remain as your friends.

Relatives—Loans from relatives also are touchy arrangements. If you do borrow from a relative, I advise that you keep it strictly on a business-like basis. Firm repayment schedule, realistic interest rate, and collateral, if possible.

Sharks—Stay from loan sharks and organized crime money. Not only are their interest rates high but non-payment of their loans can be detrimental to your health. Sometimes they will even have you take out a life insurance policy on yourself with them named as beneficiary. If something happens and you can't pay them back, then something else is likely to happen—namely, to you.

Life Insurance Policy Loans—An excellent source. Loans are on the cash surrender values of life insurance policies. Unfortunately, life insurance cash values often don't amount to much.

Your Trade Account Creditors—A lot of people borrow, in effect, from their suppliers and other creditors by paying them late. You can only work trade credit so far and usually it is only a month or two before they start harrassing you for their money. Sometimes a major supplier will help a beginning small businessman out by giving him 60 days or more to pay instead of the normal 30 days. It's worth a try to hit your suppliers up for extended credit. Sometimes they will help you out getting started in hopes that you will eventually become a large customer.

Sell Stock in Your Own Company—Earlier I indicated that small businesses can't raise money by selling their capital stock. That statement isn't entirely true. Sometimes a small businessman can manage to sell some in small private offerings. Normally, though, most people just aren't interested in becoming minority stockholders in small companies.

Factoring Your Receivables—Factoring is where you sell your receivables to a finance company. Factoring is expensive. The finance company charges a lot because it has to take over the problem of collecting the receivables and it assumes the risk of bad debts. There is a bad connotation to factoring that may be damaging to your reputation. Customers usually don't like to have their accounts sold to a finance company. In addition, if your suppliers find out about it, they may take it as being an indication that you are in trouble and limit their credit to you.

Flooring —This is where you borrow money from a bank or a finance company on your inventory. Promissory notes are created listing specific inventory items as collateral. As soon as a floored inventory item is sold, its portion of the loan, plus interest must be immediately paid. To make sure the borrower actually pays off his flooring when inventory is sold, the lender periodically conducts a "flooring check." That is, the lender actually visits the borrower's store and physically verifies that the unpaid inventory items on his outstanding flooring notes are still in inventory. Because of all the handling and processing costs, flooring is expensive borrowing.

Equipment Loans—If you have heavy equipment purchases to make, they can usually be financed for from three to five years through either the equipment manufacturer himself or the bank. The equipment itself serves as collateral via a chattel mortgage. Interest on equipment loans is normally fairly high. Down payments of 20% to 33-1/3% are usually required.

Equipment Leases—If you can't come up with the necessary down payment for an equipment loan, then you may be able to lease it. The interest cost built into equipment leases is extremely high. You should lease only if your working capital is so low you can't acquire the equipment any other way.

That's about it. As you can see, small businesses have a problem. Most of their money sources involve high interest costs and short repayment terms.

Here is the experience one small businesswoman recently had, as related to the business editor of a major newspaper:

> There just didn't seem to be any good answers to her questions. "Why is it that they all want to control the company if they make an investment in it?" she asked. "I'm willing to make a fair deal, but they want it all."

> Mrs. Wolfe and fourteen fellow stockholders had put up $156,000 in total. She watched outgo exceeding income and sought additional financing. Banks turned her down because she had no proven history of earnings. Mrs. Wolfe went to one small business investment company after another. One asked for 40%

of the equity ownership of the firm in exchange for $7,000. Another asked for 50% of the gross; still another, 65% of the net. All required the firm's assets be pledged against the note. She said: "That's impossible to live with. I'm willing to give proper security but they shouldn't become equity owners without equity shares. But they want to control the company. It's just wrong. There must be some agency in the area that doesn't need control of the company to put some money into it."

Maybe. Maybe not. She hasn't been able to find one.

23

Your Friendly Banker

If you invest your tuppance, wisely in
   the bank,
   Safe and sound,
Soon that tuppance, safely, invested in
   the bank,
   Will com-pound!
And you'll achieve that sense of conquest,
   As your aff-lu-ence expands,
In the hands of thee directors,
   Who invest as pro-pri-ety demands.*

The Banker in *Mary Poppins*

I always thought Jesus had the right idea when he drove the
money changers out of the temple. I've never much cared for
bankers either. It has been said that a banker is someone who
loans you an umbrella when the sun is shining and takes it away
from you when it starts to rain.

I've often thought if I could collect all the nation's bankers in
a big gunny sack out in the middle of the ocean, that I would
jump overboard with the sack and sacrifice myself just to rid the
world of them.

*" Fidelity Fiduciary Bank," ©1963, 1965 Wonderland Music Co. Words
and Music by Richard M. & Robert B. Sherman.

Unfortunately, banks are the biggest source of outside capital a small businessman has, so somehow you have to learn to live with them. I suppose it's possible. If we can reach an accommodation with Red China then I guess it's conceivable we can co-exist with banks.

The first thing you have to get through your head, though, is that the bank really doesn't want to loan you (the small businessman), any money. Put yourself in the bank's place. Suppose you had $1,000,000 to lend out. Which would you rather do—make ten $100,000 loans or, one hundred $10,000 loans? At first impulse, you might be inclined to think that having $1,000,000 spread out over 100 small loans would be a safer situation. A not-having-all-your-eggs-in-one-basket sort of thing.

Not so. The ten big loans are going to be just as safe, and probably safer than 100 small loans. In the first place, banks are in the position these days of being able to require about 200% collateral on loans of any consequence. So, you can safely bet that the ten $100,000 loans are going to be well-secured.

In the second place, the larger loans will be with bigger, better organized businesses whose accounting will be far superior to that of the 100 smaller borrowers. Their financial statements will be more accurate and more timely. Banks, therefore, have a better chance of keeping track of their bigger loans. It's easier for little guys to conceal problems, whether intentionally or through inadvertence.

In the third place, it's far cheaper to process and administer ten loans than it is 100, even if the total dollars lent are the same. The bank's overhead for ten big loans is a fraction of what 100 small ones cost.

In short, banks have less risk and more profit on big loans. This is why I say that they really don't want to deal with you, the small business peanut account. Now, of course, banks will officially deny this charge. You will find, however, that the man writing the bank's advertising is not the same guy who passes out its loans.

Don't ever believe anything a banker tells you. The prevailing philosophy among modern day bankers is that it is good public relations to be diplomatic. Like politicians, they hardly ever tell you what they really think, which is usually something like, "No way am I going to loan you any money, because I bet that within two years you'll be broke!"

Instead, they put on a this-hurts-me-worse-than-it-hurts-you act. They sit there grimacing and wringing their hands and saying things like, "Gee, Herb, I want to help you in the worst way and I wish to heck I could but I just can't get this by the loan committee unless you can come up with some more collateral or can produce a better looking financial statement. Do you think there's any chance you can find a relative or a friend who can invest more capital in this business? Or could you possibly find someone with a big net worth to cosign the note for you? Tell you what, why don't you come back again in a few months and we'll see if your business has gone any better. Maybe we can put something together for you then."

Banks are experts at creating conservative bureaucrats out of employees. Their technique is simple. Underlings, as a rule, are underpaid. This policy assures banks of attracting the proper wormwood type of personalities as employees. Once they are in the door, the poor devil's only hope of getting anything beyond a subsistence living is to strictly adhere to the bank's bureaucratic rules.

Eventually, if they hang on long enough, their reward will be a title of some kind plus a desk back at the home office. Junior loan officers are given enough responsibility to hang themselves. Above all else, they must never make a mistake. Even if the bank eventually recovers on its collateral, a bad loan is still a black mark on the loan officer's record.

The challenge for you, the small businessman, is to divert some of your local loan officer's loyalty from the bank to your business. How? Easy. You become his personal friend. Socialize with him. Play golf with him. Join the same service club. Have him over for dinner. Give him a fifth of whiskey for Christmas. Nobody likes to turn a friend down, not even a banker. By becoming his friend, you may pierce the veil of officialism that surrounds him. It this doesn't work, then move on to another banker and try the same routine on him. Spokesmen for banks will deny that personal friendship is a consideration in granting loans but they are lying. Many's the time I have seen loans passed out with a minimum of fuss and bother because the particular bank loan officer had known "old Pete" for 20 years and "knew" he was good for it.

The second rule is, smother the banker with paperwork. Why is it that small businessmen are so cloddish when applying for a loan? An aroma of embarrassment seems to envelop them every time they set out to borrow money. I guess it's because of the way most of us were raised. "Who goeth aborrowing, goeth a sorrowing"; "Debt is a bottomless sea"; "The Borrower is servant to the Lender," "Debt is the worst poverty." The idiotic homilies are endless. Borrowing has furtive overtones to it. For most people it's something they want to get over with as quickly and quietly as possible, like approaching a prostitute.

This attitude is a mistake. Applying for a loan should be a major production. Don't just go up to the loan officer and blurt out that you need some money. He'll just start asking you a lot of questions you aren't prepared to answer.

An experienced loan officer always suspects two things:

1. That he isn't being told half the story; and
2. That the half he is being told is only half-true.

Bankers knew what a credibility gap was long before Lyndon Johnson appeared on the scene.

So, swamp the banker with details. A mass of figures, statistics, projections, and analyses will do wonders. At a minimum, you should furnish the following:

1. Your business' balance sheet, income statement, and funds statement—preferably not more than two months old.
2. Your personal net worth statement, also not more than two months old.
3. An aged trial balance of your accounts receivable.
4. A list of major jobs in process and major orders on file.
5. An analysis of what you are going to do with the money and how you plan on paying it back.

Some sort of budget projecting next year's cash flow will be helpful too.

Now, I'm not saying the banker will actually understand all of this stuff. Bankers, as a rule, are lousy financial analysts. They know a few key "buzz" words and ratios. But having never operated a business of their own, they never quite realize what it is really all about. If you throw enough paper work at them, though, the volume alone will be enough to impress them. Occasionally you may run onto a bank that has a qualified in-house financial analyst. If this happens, change banks.

Instead of a comprehensive set of financial statements, the average small businessman walks in with a few figures he's scratched out on the back of an old envelope on the hood of his pickup truck. Naturally, the banker gives him a bad time. Meanwhile, all the glib-tongued promoters and smoothies with professional presentations are walking out of the bank's other door with thousands of loan dollars in their pockets. You've got to learn to be more like them.

Here are the major types of financing available through banks:

Self-Liquidating Loans—Banks will loan money for short terms (three months to a year) when it is for a specific purpose that will pay off the loan. In other words, if it is a self-liquidating situation. Seasonal businesses such as fruit packing and toy manufacture are classic examples; or manufacturers and contractors needing temporary financing for big jobs. The completion of the job will provide the funds necessary to pay off the loan.

Term-Loans—Banks will sometimes make installment loans of from one to five years. When they do this, they usually tie you up pretty good. You will have to agree to such things as restrictions on capital purchases, restrictions on owner's salaries, proof of adequate insurance coverage, and minimum working capital requirements.

Lines of Credit—This is an assurance (not a guarantee) that the bank will loan you money up to a predetermined set amount when and if you need it. Often the bank will require that you keep a "compensating balance" with them before they grant a line of credit. This means that you must keep a minimum amount of cash in the bank at all times. Since the bank earns money on these funds, they, in effect, are getting extra interest from you. At least once a year, you will be required to clean out line of credit loans (reduce them to zero).

Receivable Loans—Banks usually will loan you money on your receivables. Under this arrangement, you furnish them with copies of your current accounts receivable. As you collect these receivables, you are then obliged to turn the proceeds over to the bank.

Flooring—Banks will make inventory loans on a flooring basis. Flooring, you remember, is where they loan on specific inventory items. As inventory items are sold, their respective flooring loans must be immediately paid off.

Equipment Loans—You can finance equipment purchases through a bank. These are similar to automobile loans. The bank holds a chattel mortgage on the equipment as collateral.

Security Requirements—If you are a small operator, the bank just flat out isn't going to trust you very far. If you ask for a loan of any consequence, you will have to put up collateral, such as blanket liens on inventories, or second mortgages on real estate. If you have any private investments in the stock market, the bank may want the stock certificates assigned to them as collateral. If your business is a corporation, you will have to personally guarantee all of its loans. (This is why the limited liability feature of a corporation doesn't mean much if it is a small business).

Bank money is basically short term money. That is, you have to keep it revolving. You have to keep paying it back in a year or two. And it is costly. One way or another the bank is going to get 8% to 12% out of you. But there isn't much choice. Nobody accumulates enough to completely finance his own business. Eventually we all must visit our "friendly" neighborhood banker. So, it's best that you make your peace with him at the start. The Devil must have his due.

24

Uncle Sam Loves You!
Signed,
the S. B. A.

It seems that the best that any modern political
system can hope for is to use right-wing methods to
implement left-wing policies. It is a difficult trick to
pull off and requires great professional finesse, not to
mention double-talk. If modern politicians are frequently the subject of scorn and satire, it's because
too many people see through the trick too often. But
given the size of the present super-tribes there appears
to be no alternative.*

> Desmond Morris,
> *The Human Zoo*

I'm not the first guy to come along and point out that small
business has problems. Other people have been saying the same
thing for years. As a matter of fact, Congress became concerned

*From *The Human Zoo* by Desmond Morris. Copyright 1969, McGraw
Hill Book Company. Used with permission of McGraw-Hill Book Company.

during the 1950's to the point where it felt the Federal government should get into the act. So Congress created the Small Business Administration.

The S.B.A.'s mission was to gallop all over the countryside rescuing small businesses from oblivion. This it was supposed to do by loaning money to those not able to borrow from conventional sources and by passing out free management advice and technical information.

It has been a noble effort but an ineffectual one. Lending money and giving advice to small businesses doesn't equalize the basic imbalance of power. It's like giving blood transfusions and shots of Novocaine to a featherweight boxer so he can continue to have his brains beat out by Muhammad Ali. The real problem, you see, is that Big Business has an enormous built-in competitive advantage caused by the very fact of its size alone.

The only way things can really be equalized is to make Big Business compete with an arm and a leg tied behind its back. Either that or else give small business a sledgehammer and a stepladder. However, complaining about the way things are doesn't accomplish anything. The S.B.A. is a lot better than nothing and should be utilized whenever possible. The following are various services offered by the S.B.A.

Business Loans

As mentioned before, the S.B.A. does loan money, usually in the form of guarantees for regular bank loans. S.B.A. business loans are for the expansion and development of a business. The funds can't be used to pay off existing creditors, can't be distributed to the owners or used to replace funds previously distributed to the owners, can't be used for speculation of any kind, and can't be used to buy an existing business or an ownership in an existing business. The S.B.A. has a tendency to look favorably upon loans that will result in increased employment for the local economy. It also helps if your business is in an economically depressed region.

Construction loans can be for up to 15 years. Working capital loans are limited to no more than six years. The S.B.A. can go three different ways on a loan:

a. The S.B.A. can guarantee bank loans. Their guarantee can be for up to 90% of the bank's loan with a maximum ceiling of $350,000. These are sweet deals for the banks. Banks get to charge pretty much the regular going rates of interest even though 90% of their money is backed by the Federal government. In addition, S.B.A. guaranteed loans don't reduce the bank's borrowing power with the Federal Reserve.

b. The S.B.A. can participate in the loan. Here the S.B.A. puts up part of the money (limited to $150,000) and the bank puts up the rest. The S.B.A. charges a low interest rate for its portion of the loan.

c. The S.B.A. can loan directly. If no bank is willing to go in on the deal, then the S.B.A. will consider loaning all of the money itself (maximum of $100,000). These are good deals for the small business borrower because S.B.A.'s interest rate is lower than the banks. Direct loans, however, are rare. Normally there aren't enough Federal funds available for the S.B.A. to grant many.

Economic Opportunity Loans

These are loans to small businesses owned by the disadvantaged (translated = minority races). These loans are for up to $15,000 for a maximum of 15 years at low interest rates. In severely depressed areas (slums and ghettos) interest rates can be reduced to 4%. Along with the loan, the S.B.A. also provides counseling and management training. Viet Nam veterans now get special consideration under this category of loans.

Natural Disaster Loans

When floods, earthquakes, or hurricanes strike, the S.B.A. goes in afterwards and makes loans to repair the damage. Interest is only 3% and terms are for as long as 30 years. Private homeowners and churches are eligible as well as businesses.

Economic-Injury Loans

The S.B.A. loans money to small firms that have been damaged from such things as forced relocation due to urban renewal or highway construction programs; major or natural disasters; U.S. trade agreements; or food spoilage and livestock diseases.

S.C.O.R.E.

S.C.O.R.E. is an S.B.A. sponsored group of retired executives who offer free advice and counseling to small businesses. Supposedly, the small business owner receives seasoned advice from experienced experts. I've never known any one who has actually consulted S.C.O.R.E. so I can't comment on the quality of its services. All I can do is point out its existence. See your local S.B.A. office for details.

Publications

Several hundred booklets and pamphlets are available through the S.B.A. The topics and subjects are varied but generally they have to do with managing a small business. They are brief, non-technical, and easy to read. Here are a few titles selected at random to give you some idea of their diversity:

>Problems in Managing a Family-Owned Business
>Using Census Data in Small Plant Marketing
>Guidelines for Building a New Plant
>Keeping Machines and Operations Productive
>How to Analyze Your Own Business
>PERT/CPM Management System for the Small Subcontractor
>Handicrafts and Home Businesses
>Outwitting Bad Check-Passers
>Controlling Inventory in Small Wholesale Firms
>Starting and managing a Retail Flower Shop
>A Survey of Federal Government Publications of Interest to
>Small Business
>Using Weather Services in Your Business
>Economical Chip Breakers for Machining Steel
>Easy-to-Make Flip Charts Provide Selling Tools

Many S.B.A. publications are free. Prices for the others range from 20¢ to $1.25. Consult your local S.B.A. office for a complete list of what is available.

S.B.I.C.'s

The S.B.A. helps finance the Small Business Investment Companies as discussed earlier. S.B.I.C.'s remember, provide equity capital and long-term loans to small businesses. As I've said before, I'm cool on them. My impression is that they take several pounds of flesh for whatever money they give you.

L.D.C.'s

The S.B.A. also helps organize and finance Local Development Companies. These are companies set up to bring new industry into local communities. L.D.C.'s construct such things as shopping centers and industrial parks and then lease or sell the facilities to small businesses.

Individual Counseling

The folks are friendly down at your local S.B.A. office. Informality is emphasized. If you wander in to one of their offices, chances are there will always be a loan officer available to discuss your problems with. This can be helpful because most S.B.A. personnel have had extensive previous experience in private business. Every city of any consequence has a local S.B.A. field office. Don't be bashful about visiting them. They are there to help you, the little guy, and they do try. If nothing else, you'll receive sympathy for your problems.

The S.B.A. isn't the only governmental agency loaning money. Here, briefly, are some other sources:

1. *Defense Production Guarantees*—It's possible to have loans guaranteed by the Federal government if they are for operations deemed essential to the country's national defense (i.e., companies doing business with the Armed Services, N.A.S.A., G.S.A., A.E.C., or Defense Supply Agency).

2. *Shipbuilding*—The Maritime Administration helps finance construction and reconstruction of vessels for private shipowners.

3. *Agricultural Loans*—The Department of Agriculture has a whole potful of programs for farmers. They loan money for such things as buying farms, improving farms, buying farm equipment, soil and water conservation, rural water and sewer systems, irrigation projects, farm labor housing, disasters, watershed development, refinancing of existing debts, and financing of production. See your local Farmers Home Administration Office for specific information.

4. *Veterans*—The Veterans Administration makes business loans to veterans through banks and private lenders. Check with your local V.A. for eligibility requirements.

5. *Bureau of Indian Affairs*—Indians, Eskimos, and Aleuts can borrow money from the Bureau for income producing enterprises.

6. *Fisheries*—Financing can be had through the Bureau of Fisheries for buying, constructing, equipping, repairing, maintaining, or operating commercial fishing vessels and fishing gear.

7. *Overseas Private Investment Corporation (O.P.I.C.)*—O.P.I.C. provides services for those U.S. citizens or companies interested in setting up businesses in underdeveloped foreign countries. Besides financing, the O.P.I.C. also provides counseling and insurance against war, revolution, and expropriation.

8. *Export-Import Operations*—The Export-Import Bank of the United States assists in the financing of U.S. foreign trade. Among other things, the Export-Import Bank loans money to overseas buyers of U.S. goods and guarantees and insures U.S. exporters against foreign commercial and political risks.

9. *F.H.A. Loans*—The Federal Housing Administration insures mortgages and loans of property owners, lessees, investors, builders, and developers. F.H.A. insured loans are used for such things as mobile homes, apartment houses, duplexes, housing for the elderly, and housing for low-income families. The F.H.A. also provides rent supplements for low-income families.

There, you see? I bet you didn't know the Federal Government actually cared, did you?

25

Tax Shelters

"How come YOU don't know any tax
loopholes?"

Newspapers and magazines make it tough for us C.P.A.'s. They are forever publishing lurid articles about tax shelters and tax loopholes and how rich people never have to pay income tax because of all the gimmicks set up for them by the smart C.P.A.'s and lawyers they hire. Naturally, these subjects make for high readership interest. Unfortunately, most of them are misleading.

Clients are always reading tax loophole type articles and then coming in and asking me why-n-hell I don't set them up so they don't have to pay any taxes either? They wave some magazine article in front of my face and accuse me of falling down on the job. "Why don't you do something like that for me? I mean, after all, that's what I'm paying you for, isn't it? To cut down on my taxes?" So I sit the guy down and patiently explain to him how the particular article he read was grossly oversimplified, didn't explain all of the facts, did not point out the drawbacks, and was mostly designed to titillate the reader rather than to pass on accurate information.

The trouble is, clients never quite believe this. Tax deductions are like sex—everyone suspects he is getting less than the next guy. Give a put-down explanation of tax shelters to a client and more than likely he suspects that you are some kind of a hick who doesn't know all of the tricks and gimmicks used by sophisticated C.P.A.'s. Or else he suspects that you aren't telling him everything—as though there is some kind of a secret tax loophole club that he is being left out of.

Well sit up and pay attention, kiddies, because I am now going to explain the facts of life to you about tax shelters and tax loopholes. I mean, what they are really all about and not what some promoter using them as a cloak for his own interests would like to have you believe.

First of all, you've got to understand that United States tax laws (Code, Regulations, Rulings, and Court Cases) constitute the most complicated, fouled up hodgepodge of verbiage existent in the English language. Even Einstein claimed he could never understand a U.S. income tax return.

Tax laws have grown in bits and pieces over the last 60 years. They are the patchwork product of the pressures, hastes, and compromises of thousands of lobbyists, special interest groups, politicians, and government lawyers. The collection of revenues is only incidental to their major purposes which are to achieve various and sundry economic, social, demographic, foreign trade, ecological, political and special interest goals. Congress changes them every year, the I.R.S. changes them every month, and the Courts change them every day. There is just no way anyone can give a simple, comprehensive layman's explanation of them without being at least partially misleading.

You think I'm laying it on a bit thick? OK, try this on for size. It is part of just *one* sentence from I.R.S. Code, Section 341 (e)(1):

> For purposes of subsection (a) (1), a corporation shall not be considered to be a collapsible corporation with respect to any sale or exchange of stock of the corporation by a shareholder if, at the time of such sale or exchange, the sum of (A) the net realized appreciation in subsection (3) assets of the corporation (as defined in Paragraph (5) (A)), plus (B) if the shareholder owns more than 5 percent in value of the outstanding stock of the corporation, the net unrealized appreciation in assets of the corporation (other than assets described in subparagraph (A)) which would be subsection (3) assets under clauses (i) and (iii) of paragraph (5) (A) if the shareholder owned more than 20 percent in value of such stock plus (C) if the shareholder owns more than 20 percent in value of the outstanding stock of the corporation and owns, or at any time during the preceding 3-year period more than 20 percent in value of the outstanding stock of any other corporation more than 70 percent in value of the assets of which are, or were at any time during which such shareholder owned during such 3-year period more than 20 percent in value of the outstanding stock, assets similar to related in service or use to assets comprising more than 60 percent in value of the assets of the corporation, the net unrealized appreciation in assets of . . .

Now, isn't that just priceless? It continues on like that for another 243 words. Total sentence length—474 words! There are even longer examples elsewhere in the Code. Sentences of 100 to 200 words are commonplace.

Or, how about a quadruple negative? Section 205(f):

> A plan shall not be treated as not satisfying the requirements of this section solely because, under the plan there is a provision that any election under subsection (c) or (3), and any revocation of any such election, does not become effective (or ceases to be effective) if the participant dies within a period (not in excess of 2 years) beginning on the date of such election or revocation, as the case may be.

Naturally, no layman can hope to understand this sort of crap. To meet the need for interpretations, a whole new guild of pedants has arisen. They are known as "tax advisors." They earn their livelihood by explaining the income tax law's foggybottom complexities to laymen. For specific advice concerning a specific factual situation, you will have to consult one of them. All I intend to get across here is the general picture.

There are three basic ways to save on income taxes:

1. Convert taxable income into non-taxable income.
2. Defer taxable income until a later year.
3. Get income into a lower tax bracket.

Every tax shelter, every tax loophole, every tax saving scheme known to man is a variation of one of these three methods. Here are the specific techniques still available under each method as of this writing. *Note: Because tax laws change so rapidly, by the time you read this there will undoubtedly be differences in current tax rules. Consequently, I can not over-emphasize the importance of seeking professional advice before trying to apply anything mentioned in this book.*

A. Converting Taxable Income into Non-Taxable Income

There are a few ways that you can actually earn money without paying tax on it.

1. Tax-Free Municipal Bonds

Interest received on bonds issued by states and municipalities is tax free. Rich people usually buy lots of municipal bonds. If you are in the 65% tax bracket, receiving 4-1/2% interest tax free on a municipal is like getting 13% interest anywhere else.

Drawbacks—Bonds are long-term investments. It takes years for them to mature. They can be sold privately prior to maturity, but you may have to take a discount to do so. Bonds normally don't appreciate in value. This means you lose part of your investment to inflation during the time you hold them. Interest rates on municipals are lower than commercial bonds. The advantage from their tax free character falls off rapidly as you get down into the lower tax brackets. For a 25% tax bracket investor,

4-1/2% interest on a municipal is like receiving 6% taxable interest. That is a far cry from the equivalent 13% interest a 65% tax bracket gets. Finally, if you borrow money to buy tax free municipals, you don't get to deduct the loan interest.

2. Oil Depletion

22% of the gross income from oil and gas wells is tax free. This is the celebrated oil depletion allowance. Oil depletion is a tremendous tax break for those companies in the business. Depletion allowances are also available for other minerals at lesser rates. In recent years, promoters have organized partnerships in oil and gas ventures to make the tax advantages available to investors. Investors' money is used to explore for new oil and gas wells. Most of the costs of this exploration are deductible and, if oil or gas is discovered, 22% of the gross income is excluded from tax. The 1975 Tax Reduction Act, however, limits depletion to small producers only. In addition, standing in 1981, 22% rate is scaled down each year until it reaches 15% by 1984.

Drawbacks - You don't get tax free income from oil depletion unless you receive income in the first place. Oil depletion is no tax shelter *until* you have producing wells. The tax advantages of the Dry Hole Oil Company are illusionary. Exploring for oil is a very risky business. Enormous capital investment and technical know-how are required. The chances of an ordinary taxpayer being able to cash in on oil depletion are slim. Investing in an oil and gas partnership means you are entrusting your money to complete strangers for operations carried on many miles away. The financing is complicated. Even if oil is found, it is possible for the general partner to siphon off excessive management fees, costs, and other loading charges without your ever being aware of it. Many investment syndicates for outsiders are wildcatting operations with little chance of actually hitting a producing well.

3. Corporate Fringe Benefits

Corporations have several fringe benefits they can pass on to employees that are deductible to the corporation and tax free to the employees:

a. *$5,000 Widows Death Benefit*—Corporations can give widows of deceased employees up to $5,000 tax free.

Drawbacks—You have to die in order to get it.

b. *Employees Medical Expenses*—Corporations can pay an employee's medical expenses, tax free to the employee.

Drawbacks—You have to become sick in order to obtain the benefits. Also, you may have to include other employees besides yourself in the plan (assuming you are the owner of the corporation). The cost of paying medical expenses for other employees may be enough to wipe out the tax advantages.

c. *Group Term Life Insurance*—Corporations can pay the premiums on group term life insurance policies for employees on up to $50,000 of life insurance.

Drawbacks—You have to include other employees besides yourself in order to make up the "group." The cost of their policies offsets your tax advantage.

d. *Sick Pay*—Up to $100 a week of salary paid while absent from work for medical reasons can be excluded from tax.

Drawbacks—You have to become sick in order to get it and there is a waiting period before the exclusion applies.

4. Excess Deductions for Business Expenses

Some business deductions can be taken even though they exceed actual costs!

a. *Auto Mileage*—You can deduct 15¢ a mile as auto expense for business purposes on the first 15,000 of business miles driven and 10¢ a mile for all miles driven thereafter. You get these deductions even if actual expenses are less.

Drawbacks—You must maintain very good mileage records in order to support the deduction. The tax benefits in excess of cost really don't amount to an awful lot when all is said and done.

b. *Vacation While on Business Trips*—The costs of traveling to and from a business destination are deductible even though you take a vacation along the way, provided the "primary" reason for making the trip was for business. On overseas trips, travel costs must be allocated between business and pleasure if the trip is for more than one week and less than 75% of the time is spent on business.

Drawbacks—You have to keep good records of your activities. The amount of tax benefit usually doesn't amount to an awful lot. By the time your wife gets through spending money on shopping trips, you'll probably lose in the end.

5. Tax Free Income Earned Abroad

You don't have to pay U.S. income tax on the first $20,000 of income earned in foreign countries as long as you are absent from the United States 17 out of 18 months. If you stay away three full years, you get to exclude $25,000 a year.

Drawbacks—You have to be a semi-exile in order to qualify and you are subject to whatever income taxes the foreign country you reside in assesses. Many countries have higher income tax rates than the U.S., believe it or not. Besides, it's pretty hard to earn as much in a foreign country as you would here, unless maybe you are a movie star.

6. Hobby Losses

Losses incurred in so-called hobbies such as farming or horse racing can be deducted even though you have another trade or business as your primary source of income.

Drawbacks—You have to have profits in two out of five years in order to deduct the losses (two out of seven years in the case of horse racing). You have to able to show that the "hobby" is actually being run with the intention of making profits. Often the losses are "real" losses even after tax rebates.

7. Intercompany Dividends

85% of the dividends received by one corporation from another are tax free. Hence, if your corporation holds your personal stock investments, it will pay tax on only 15% of any dividends received.

Drawbacks—If dividends and other passive-type income get to be too large a part of your corporation's income, you may run afoul of the "personal holding company" statutes. If this happens, you will be stuck for a special penalty tax. Besides, intercorporate dividends are, in effect, ultimately taxed. Stockholders ultimately pay tax if they take the money out of the corporation or if they sell their corporation. Also, if your corporation should happen to lose money on its stock investments, the losses can't be deducted unless there are subsequent capital gains.

8. Sale of Residence After Age 65

If you sell your house after you hit 65, any gain attributable to the first $20,000 of sale price is tax free.

Drawbacks—Who wants to be 65?

9. Charitable Gifts of Appreciated Property

Suppose you pledged $500 to the church. Instead of cash, you could give the church capital stock certificates worth $500. If the stock's $500 value is more than your cost, you don't have to pay any tax on the gain. *Example:* You give the church stock worth $500 but it only cost you $200 six months ago. You get a $500 deduction and you don't have to pay tax on the $300 appreciation.

Drawbacks—This applies only to intangible property and real estate. You save taxes *only* if you had intended to make a gift in the first place.

10. Gifts of a Future Interest

It is possible to donate your house or your farm to a charity and still retain the use of it until you die. If properly executed, you get a tax deduction for the present value of your house or farm, after allowing for depreciation based on your estimated life span.

Drawbacks—This means a charity winds up with your house or farm instead of your children or other heirs. By the time you allow for depreciation and present values, the amount of deduction diminishes substantially. You lose control of your house or farm while you are alive by not being able to sell it.

11. Life Insurance Proceeds Received in Installments by a Surviving Spouse

If you die, your spouse can elect to receive your life insurance proceeds in installments rather than in a lump sum. If so, the life insurance company pays an additional amount above and beyond the actual policy proceeds. This represents interest on the retained funds. Up to $1,000 a year of this excess is tax free.

Drawbacks—You have to die in order to receive the benefit. Your spouse may be able to earn more money on the insurance proceeds than the insurance company.

12. Investment Tax Credit

If you buy equipment used in your business, you get a tax credit of up to 10% of its purchase price.

Drawbacks—To get the credit, you have to buy something. 10% isn't enough to warrant buying equipment unless you need the equipment in the first place.

13. 20% Job Development Tax Credit

If you employ persons participating in the federal government's Work Incentive Program (W.I.N.), you are entitled to a tax credit amounting to 20% of their first year's wages. (W.I.N. is a federal program aimed at finding jobs and training for welfare recipients).

Drawbacks—There are no tax drawbacks. However, I suspect you'll probably have a tough time finding competent employees among the W.I.N. program. Furthermore, you have to keep W.I.N. employees on the payroll for at least two years or else you have to pay back the credit.

14. Western Hemisphere Trade Corporation

A Western Hemisphere Trade Corporation is a U.S. corporation that derives at least 95% of its gross income from sources outside the United States, from either North, South or Central America, or from the West Indies. Western Hemisphere Trade Corporations get a special for-them-only deduction of approximately 29%.

Drawbacks—None, if you can qualify, but how many businesses do you know that can?

15. Cheat

It doesn't take some people very long to figure out that one sure-fire way to save taxes is to simply not report all of their income in the first place. In other words, they cheat! This is most prevalent in businesses that handle cash—such as taverns, barbershops, restaurants, motels, etc.

In those instances where it is done, cash is taken out of the till without being recorded on the books of account. This is known as "skimming" or "creaming" in the trade. Now I don't condone this sort of activity, nor do I suggest that cheating is a bona fide tax saving method. I list it here for academic purposes only because it is, in fact, a technique used by some people.

Drawbacks—First, you will feel guilty, which is an uncomfortable state of mind to be in. Second, you will suffer from the worry of being caught. Third, you may actually be caught.

The I.R.S. is painfully aware of the fact that cheating does go on. They also know the types of situations where it usually occurs. They have special agents who do nothing but investigate suspected cheaters. The I.R.S. has unlimited time and resources available to it for smoking out a suspect. They won't hesitate to use them either. The I.R.S. doesn't care about making money on fraud cases. All they want to do is make an example out of the guy in hopes that the ensuing publicity will scare other taxpayers out of trying the same thing.

I've seen a number of people go through tax fraud investigations and I'm here to tell you that it isn't worth it. If you are a crook to begin with, that is one thing. But most tax fraud cases involve taxpayers who are nice, decent people in all other respects. The humiliation and pressure of a fraud investigation literally takes years off their lives. Since they aren't by nature crooks, psychologically they wind up dying a thousand deaths.

The Internal Revenue Service has various means at its disposal for proving fraud. A standard method is to "net worth" the suspect. "Net worthing" means the I.R.S. figures out the increase in a taxpayer's net assets from the beginning of the year to the end of the year. Then they add in the taxpayer's estimated living expenses for the year. This total represents the taxpayer's approximate income. If less than this has been reported on his tax return, the taxpayer has some explaining to do.

If you cheat long enough, chances are someone besides the I.R.S. will find out about it. The I.R.S. pays a 10% finder's fee to informers. This gets them lots of tips in situations they ordinarily would not uncover.

From time to time, the I.R.S. conducts special fishing expeditions to look for specific instances of fraud. Last year, for example, in my hometown, the I.R.S. visited all those businesses known to be purchasers of scrap metal. They then examined the cancelled checks that these firms used to pay for their scrap metal purchases. Every time they came upon a cancelled check endorsed as having been cashed for money rather than being deposited, they wrote down the name of the payee. Then they checked that person's records to see if he had reported the scrap sales on his tax return.

Many people feel that a significant amount of skimming still goes on despite I.R.S. efforts to clamp down on it. The problem the I.R.S. has is that "skimmers" can be difficult to detect if they are subtle, stick to cash, and don't take enough to seriously distort their income-expense ratios. Taverns and restaurants are notorious examples. Their chances of cover-up are especially good because they pay cash for so many expenses. They, therefore, can manipulate both income and expenses in such a way as to create reasonable looking income and expense ratios.

B. Defer Taxable Income to a Later Year

Most tax shelter schemes are really Faust-Mephistopheles propositions. You put off the inevitable by deferring taxes until sometime far off in the future. The advantage isn't that you actually save taxes. In the long run you may even pay more. The advantage is that, during the deferral period, you have the use of the deferred tax money. Hopefully, you will be able to earn income on it during that interim.

1. Qualified Pension and Profit Sharing Plans

Money put aside each year into a pension and profit sharing plan is deductible if the plan qualifies under strict I.R.S. regulations. The amount put aside each year is deferred from taxation until the employees retire. The same goes for any income earned on the plan's trust funds. If you die before retirement, the money set aside for you is usually not subject to Federal estate tax.

Drawbacks—You have to include employees as well as yourself in such a plan in order for it to qualify under I.R.S. regulations. The plan cannot be discriminatory in favor of stockholder employees or highly paid employees. There are ways of partially getting around these restrictions, but in general, the cost of having to make contributions for employees usually more than offsets any tax advantages derived by the business owner. Money put aside in these plans is locked in until you retire. You can't get it back out before retirement even for emergencies without suffering severe tax penalties.

2. Farm Operations

Farmers have lots of opportunity for tax deferral because they aren't taxed like other people. Other businesses have to carry inventories on their books. Not farmers. They can write off the costs of planting and caring for crops immediately. Farmers are permitted to write off the costs of their cattle and chickens (unless they are for breeding purposes) rather than having to capitalize them as assets. They are permitted to write off costs of clearing and developing and improving land for farming. Non-farmers would have to capitalize such items as part of their fixed assets. Farmers are permitted to write off fertilizer and feed supplies instead of having to set them up as supply inventories. Deducting these sorts of things immediately gives farmers the use of tax dollars now rather than later.

Drawbacks—None, if you are a farmer. Small farmers, after all, need all the tax breaks they can get. Promoters, however, have gotten into the act. Farm operations for high tax bracket investors have been set up to utilize a farm operation's tax deferrals. Cattle feeding syndicates are a prime example. The trouble is that the tax advantage for investors is merely a one-year deferral. Next year the deferred income catches up to you (assuming that there is income). Next year it may be taxed at an even higher rate due to such things as the interplay of the 50% tax rate ceiling on earned income vs. the 70% maximum rate on investment income. Also, you are again entrusting your money to strangers who may nick you for extravagant operating costs.

3. Depreciation of Real Estate

Part of the cost of buildings used in your business or held for investment can be deducted each year from taxable income. This is known as "depreciation." Depreciation has to be taken back into income if the building is sold later for a profit. However, some of the depreciation recaptured may be reported as capital gains income, whereas the original deductions were against ordinary income. This means you make money on the difference between ordinary and capital gains tax rates.

Drawbacks—None, provided your building operates at a profit each year. If it doesn't, then you've got a real loss instead of a tax loss. This is the most common tax planning fallacy people fall into. They'll get their hands on some big real estate project that produces huge losses each year and they'll think, "Great, look at all the tax shelter we've got." The problem is they may be losing a lot more actual money than the tax dollars they save. It's like your wife buying a lot of clothes she doesn't need because they are on sale, then having her say: "Look at all the money I saved by buying these things on sale."

4. Intangible Drilling Costs

Intangible drilling costs (wages, fuel, supplies, repairs, etc.) incurred in drilling oil and gas wells are immediately deductible.

Drawbacks—Again, there is no tax break *unless* you hit a producing well. Otherwise the tax dollars gained from your deductions never make up for the actual costs of the drilling.

5. Installment Sales

You can defer the tax on installment sales until such time as you actually receive the installment payments. (*Note:* If what you sold was real estate or a casual sale of personal property, you cannot collect more than 30% of the sales price in the year of sale.)

Drawbacks—None, really, unless the deferral causes you to pay substantially more tax in later years than you would if you reported the gain in the year of sale. However, this isn't really a tax break. It's merely the way it should be. Why should you have to pay tax on money you haven't yet received?

6. Non-Taxable Exchanges

Two pieces of business or investment real estate can be swapped without paying tax on the exchange's gain. The exchange will be partially taxed if you receive any cash out of the deal or if you assume a smaller mortgage than the mortgage you give up. Otherwise, your gain is deferred. What happens is you reduce your tax basis in the new piece of property by the amount of gain not reported. You can also defer gain on property condemned by a public authority (such as for a highway right-of-way). On condemnation gains, you have two years in which to find a replacement for the property condemned and it must cost at least as much as the condemnation award.

On an exchange, if you can't find someone willing to trade property with you, you may be able to set up what is known as a "three party exchange." First, you find a regular buyer for your present property. Then you go out and find another piece of property you would be willing to trade your present property for. The buyer who wants your present property buys the second piece of property instead. Then he immediately turns around and exchanges it for your present property.

Drawbacks—If you swap one piece of real estate for another, then they must be equal in value. Right? If so, what have you gained? Tax free exchanges are an advantage only if you think your newly acquired property will appreciate faster than the old.

7. Prepaid Interest

It is possible to defer taxes by prepaying next year's interest on a liability. That is, assuming the creditor will accept interest paid in advance. (For him it is income acceleration rather than income deferral.)

Drawbacks—The person you pay the interest to has the use of your interest money for a year ahead of time. Therefore, in effect, you are paying about a 1% higher interest rate than if you waited and paid on time. The I.R.S. will not allow this deduction if more than one year's interest is prepaid or if the deduction materially distorts the taxpayer's income.

8. Short Sales

You can defer gain from the sale of stock until the following year by selling "short against the box." This is where you sell short but already own stock to cover the short sale with. These sales are not taxable until you actually deliver your stock to the buyer, which can be next year. This way you freeze your gain this year but defer reporting it until next year.

Drawbacks—You lose the use of the sales proceeds until you cover the short sale. In addition, you pay interest on your short sale account with the broker until the short sale is completed.

9. Foreign Tax Havens

Some foreign countries have lower tax rates than the United States. Owning a corporation in one of them makes it possible to earn and accumulate more after-tax income than in the United States. "Tax haven" income becomes taxable whenever it is brought back into this country, but up until then, U.S. taxes are deferred.

Drawbacks—In some situations, you are taxed on income of U.S. controlled foreign corporations even if the income *isn't* brought back into this country. Undistributed tax haven income becomes immediately taxable if it is from "passive" sources (dividends, rents, interest, royalties, etc.), or from profits and commissions on goods produced and sold outside of the tax haven country, or if from "services" performed for related companies. Furthermore, it isn't all that easy to set up profitable operations in tax haven countries. Many of them have shaky political systems. But if you think you can make it big as a manufacturer in Haiti, Greenland, Swaziland, or the New Hebrides, go to it.

10. Stock Options

Corporations can set up qualified stock option plans for key employees. These plans give employees the right to buy the corporation's stock sometime in the future at *today's* value. This, in effect, gives the employees a chance to earn additional compensation at capital gains rates. Corporations can also give employees a stock purchase plan allowing them to buy stock at 85% of its market value. The 15% discount is not income until the stock is ultimately sold.

Drawbacks—You have to hold stock option stock three years before it is eligible for capital gains. Qualified stock options cannot be given to any employee owning more than 10% of the corporation. The difference between the stock's option price and its fair market value is a so-called tax preference item that you may have to pay a 10% tax on.

The 15% discount on a stock purchase plan is ordinary income when the stock is sold.

Qualified stock option and stock purchase plans are of no benefit to small closely held corporations.

11. Deductions for Expenses Paid with Borrowed Money

When it comes right down to it, the biggest tax shelter going is being able to write off costs that you haven't paid for yet. This is what makes real estate so attractive. You are permitted to deduct depreciation on the balance of a real estate mortgage as well as on your equity in the property. This is where well-to-do, high tax bracket people really have something going for them. Here's an example of how this sort of thing can work out:

Daddy Bigbucks builds a two million dollar apartment house. He obtains 90% financing, so his out-of pocket costs are only $200,000. The balance ($1,800,000) is financed over 30 years at 8% interest. His apartment house operations look like this during the year:

	For Tax Purposes	In Reality
Gross rental income	$ 300,000	$ 300,000
Less 10% vacancy factor	(30,000)	(30,000)
Net rentals	$ 270,000	$ 270,000
Operating expenses (taxes, management, utilities, insurance, maintenance, etc.)	(120,000)	(120,000)
Mortgage payments	(150,000)	(150,000)
Cash flow	$ –0–	$ –0–
Equity portion of mortgage payment	$ 10,000	$ 10,000
Depreciation write-offs (using accelerated methods)	(70,000)	
Tax loss	$(60,000)	
Taxes saved by applying $60,000 loss against Bigbuck's other income		$ 30, 000
Actual After-Tax Profit		$ 40,000

Really amazing, isn't it? Bigbuck's apartment house only breaks even as far as cash flow goes. Yet, because of big depreciation write-offs, Bigbucks receives $30,000 in cash from tax rebates.

Not only that, but his equity in the property keeps increasing each year. As a result, he makes a 20% return on his investment:

$$\frac{\$10,000 \text{ equity increase} + \$30,000 \text{ tax rebate}}{\$200,000 \text{ original investment}} = 20\% \text{ return}$$

Now, of course, his tax benefits keep decreasing every year because mortgage interest and depreciation keep declining. But for five or ten years anyway, Bigbucks makes cash profits solely because of his tax deductions.

Pretty slick, eh? In later years when the apartment starts throwing off profits instead of tax losses, Bigbucks pyramids up by starting another project. He uses his accumulated tax rebates and the equity in his first apartment to help finance the second.

What makes all of this possible is the opportunity to do two things:

1. To deduct depreciation on something that isn't, in fact, depreciating at all; and

2. To depreciate not only the cash invested in a piece of property, but also what is owed on the mortgage.

Drawbacks—This scheme works beautifully so long as everything goes according to plan. But sometimes things can go wrong. For example, suppose the vacancy rate hits 20% instead of 10% and suppose the apartment house doesn't retain its value and suppose its operating expenses are 20% greater than what Bigbucks counted on? Then, instead of breaking even it will show a *negative* cash flow of $54,000. In other words, Bigbucks would have to dump $54,000 a year into it just to pay its expenses. However, as long as Bigbucks stays in a high tax bracket, like 50% or 60%, he still comes out all right. This is so because his tax rebates from the increased losses jump to $57,000 leaving a $3,000 after-tax cash flow. But suppose Bigbucks isn't in the 50% tax bracket anymore? Suppose he has so many losses that he drops down into the 30% bracket? Then he will have a $20,000 after-tax *cash loss* instead of a gain. And suppose Bigbucks can't come up with the money to pay for these losses?

What I'm getting at is that this sort of thing is mainly for the big boys. Trying to duplicate it on a small scale can get you into trouble. Suppose you did what Bigbucks did but on a one-tenth scale? That is, you built a $200,000 apartment instead of a

$2,000,000 apartment. It still would be necessary to come up with $20,000 cash in order to swing the deal. Not many small businessmen have that much change lying around. Even if you do, your tax benefits will not be as great, proportionately, as for Bigbucks. Being in, say, the 25% bracket, your tax rebate is only $1,500 instead of the $3,000 it would be if you were in the 50% bracket. This only gives you a 12-1/2% return vs. Bigbucks' 20%.

A 12-1/2% return still isn't bad, but if you run into the same kind of vacancy and operating expense troubles Bigbucks had, you will suffer a $4,500 after-tax cash loss instead of a cash profit. Furthermore, your tax rebate doesn't come until after you've filed your annual income tax return. In the meantime, you would have had to carry a $6,000 cash loss for the year. Other drawbacks, under *certain* circumstances, are that the fast depreciation write-offs can be subject to a special 10% "tax preference" tax and up to one-half of the mortgage interest can be disallowed as a deduction.

12. Tax Deferral Accounting Methods

When you start out in business, there are several accounting methods you can elect to use that will defer taxes:

a. Cash method accounting (available only to businesses that don't carry inventories).

b. Bad debt reserves (allows you to deduct estimated bad debts before they occur).

c. Accelerated depreciation (enables you to obtain most of your depreciation deduction early in the life of an asset).

d. LIFO inventories (allows you to value inventories at "old" historical costs).

e. Having your accounting year end on some date other than December 31 (such an election is available only to corporations unless you have prior I.R.S. approval).

Drawbacks—None, usually.

13. D.I.S.C. (Domestic International Sales Corp.)

D.I.S.C.'s are export corporations that derive at least 95% of their income from sales to foreign countries. To stimulate export activity, the United States exempts 50% of a D.I.S.C. corporation's income from tax. D.I.S.C. stockholders get taxed on this deferred undistributed income only when they sell or dispose of their D.I.S.C. stock.

Drawbacks—There aren't any, tax-wise. But it's not an easy thing to find products you can sell profitably overseas. Would you like trying to sell binoculars or transistor radios to Japan? Or how about toys to Taiwan? You think maybe you could sell Detroit automobiles in Europe? How about hotdogs in Argentina? For most people, creating a D.I.S.C. is like flying to the moon.

14. Low Income Housing Rehabilitation Cost Write-Offs

Here, at last, is a real boondoggle! Low Income Housing Rehabilitation projects (known as Rehabs) are Federally subsidized housing programs for low income people. Rehabs usually work this way: A contractor gets together with a group of high tax bracket investors. Together they buy an old run-down hotel or apartment building. Next, they obtain approval from the F.H.A. to rebuild it and convert it into housing for low income renters. The F.H.A. gives the group a 40-year mortgage for 90% of the project's total cost (including the original cost of the building). The investors put up the other 10%. When completed, the F.H.A. subsidizes up to 70% of the rents of the low income occupants. Investors are allowed only a 6% cash return on their investment but they are not personally liable on either the mortgage or on any negative cash flow. The blockbuster is that the I.R.S. permits the investors to write off the rehabilitation costs over just 5 years. Rehabilitation costs usually amount to one-half to three-fourths of the Rehab's total costs, so the tax write-off is enormous. A person in the 50% tax bracket can get two or three times his orginal investment back within five years just from the tax deductions alone!

The end result, after the smoke has cleared, is this:

a. The contractor makes a profit from rehabilitating the property plus he gets a fee for managing it after it is completed;

b. The investors get at least two or three times their original investment back in tax rebates plus a possible 6% annual cash flow;

c. The low income renters get excellent housing for ridiculously low rents; and

   d. The taxpayers, meaning good old middle-class you and I, pay for it all.

   Many Rehab projects have been created in undesirable, crime-ridden urban areas. These particular projects have had trouble attracting enough renters to make the mortgage payments. This means they may eventually have to be repossessed by the government. Since the investors aren't liable on the mortgage, they can just walk away from the project. The result is that, after the contractor has made a nice profit on the construction and after the fat cat investors have made a nice profit on their write-offs, Uncle Sam is left holding the bag.

   When the true costs of Rehab projects finally become known to the taxpayers, a lot of people are going to be awfully mad. In the meantime, Rehabs make just great tax shelters. There just doesn't seem to be any way a high tax bracket investor can be seriously hurt in them. This is so because the investor's profit is from tax deductions, not the project's cash flow. Not being personally liable for either the mortgage or negative cash flow, his risk is confined to his 10% investment. I understand that some wealthy investors have standing offers with real estate brokers to buy all the Rehab projects they can get their hands on, sight unseen.

   Drawbacks—Well, I guess there is one way you can lose on a Rehab. If the F.H.A. does repossess for nonpayment on the mortgage, the investors will have to report as income all the previous fast write-off deductions they've taken. In addition, they will lose whatever actual cash they have invested in the project, to the extent it hasn't been recouped by cash flow. However, the real estate men I've talked to about this don't seem to think that repossession is a very likely possibility. They feel that the government is reluctant to repossess Rehabs. First of all, the government isn't anxious for it to be known that many Rehabs are failures. Second, the government doesn't particularly want to get into the business of managing low income apartment houses that are in trouble. The last thing the government wants to be is a slum landlord.

   Another problem with Rehabs is that, naturally, promoters have gotten into the act. Promoters have been putting together deals where they load in heavy consulting costs and finder's fees.

Also, the promoters may manage to take an inordinate share of the project's equity.

At the present time, the Government has a moratorium on providing funds for new Rehab projects and it now appears likely that the program will not be revived.

15. Silver Coins

This is a brand-new loophole made possible by inflation and the devaluation of the U.S. dollar. Silver coins minted prior to 1965 have increased in value because of their silver content. At the present time, coins of pre-1965 vintage can be sold to coin dealers for about three times their face value. Yet, they remain coin of the realm. Being legal tender, they are recorded at their face value for tax purposes. This means that a 1964 silver quarter is twenty-five cents for tax purposes whereas its actual value may be seventy-five cents.

I think that you can see the tax saving possibilities right away. If you receive seven hundred pre-1965 quarters, you will have gotten $525 of value, yet, you will only have to report $175 on your income tax return!

Drawbacks—First, silver coin transactions create commission expenses and holding costs that must be taken into account. Second, the coins may drop in value during the period of time that you hold them. Silver coin values are tied to the silver commodity market which fluctuates just like the stock market. Third, if you sell the the coins for money, you will be taxed on the difference between their market and face values. The tax deferral, in other words, exists only for as long as you retain possession of the coins. (The gain, though, would be captial gains if the coins were held six months). Finally, this is a fairly new concept that might be challenged by the I.R.S.

C. Getting Income Into a Lower Tax Bracket

The final tax loophole method is to somehow get your income taxed at a lower rate. In the past, the primary technique was to convert ordinary income into capital gains income. Capital gains tax rates used to be half of ordinary rates so this was quite an advantage when you could swing it. However, the tax laws have been pretty well stiffened. Converting ordinary income into capital gains income isn't quite so easy as it once was (i.e., capital gains are now restricted by such tax rules as depreciation recapture, collapsible corporation rules, restrictions on transactions between related taxpayers, special corporate distribution rules, "dealer" activities, etc.). Also, capital gains rates have been increased for high bracket taxpayers. Finally, if you have more than $30,000 of capital gains income in any one year, it is possible that you may get stuck with the new 10% minimum tax on tax preferences. Nevertheless, the following are still some possibilities for getting income taxed at lower rates.

1. Income Averaging

If your income increases substantially in one year, you can go back and "average" with the prior four years. This causes you to be taxed in a lower bracket. To be eligible for income averaging, your current year's income must be at least $3,000 more than 4/3 of your prior four year average. The actual computations are very complicated, naturally, and require a special form (Schedule G) which the I.R.S. cunningly doesn't furnish, unless you specifically ask for it. Consequently, a great many people eligible for this tax break miss out on it.

Drawbacks–None.

2. Corporate Bail Outs

Dividends received from a corporation are taxable at ordinary rates. For this reason, most people owning small corporations don't pay themselves dividends. Instead they let profits accumulate as earned surplus. As profits pile up from year to year, the corporation's net worth correspondingly increases. This makes for larger capital gains in the event the corporation is ever sold. Ultimately, stockholders can bail out their corporation's accumulated profits at capital gains rates by selling their corporation.

Drawbacks–First of all, this whole subject is academic unless your corporation is very profitable.

Second, there is a special penalty tax that can be assessed if accumulated corporate earnings exceed $150,000 and amount to more than what the reasonable needs of the business require.

Third, upon being sold, a corporation may be deemed by the I R.S. to be a so-called "collapsible corporation." If so, gain from its sale will be ordinary income rather than capital gains. Collapsible corporations are corporations whose profit from being sold comes primarily from the presence within the corporation of ordinary income-producing assets. If you think that this definition is hard to follow, then you ought to try reading the actual regulations.

3. Corporate Tax Rates

The first $25,000 of corporation profits are taxed at a flat 20% rate. The next $25,000 of corporate profits are taxed at 22%. All profits over $50,000 are taxed at 48%. Tax rates for married individuals hit 22% at $8,000 of taxable income and 48% at $40,000. By splitting income between yourself and your corporation, it is possible to save several thousand dollars of tax, if your income is high enough. Here's an example:

	Without a Corporation	With a Corporation	
		The Corp.	The Owner
Profit	$40,000	$40,000	
Owner's Salary	—	(15,000)	$15,000
Taxable Income	$40,000	$25,000	$15,000
Income Tax	$ 9,920*	$ 5,000	$ 1,820*
			$ 5,000
			1,820
Total Income Tax	$ 9,920		$ 6,820

Tax saved by being incorporated = $3,100

*Assuming joint return, standard deduction, and four exemptions.

Drawbacks—You have to leave the profits tied up within the corporation in order to save any taxes. In the long run, you may pay more tax by using a corporation. This is so because corporate income is taxed twice: once to the corporation itself, and once again to the stockholders when they take out dividends or when they sell the corporation.

4. Sale of Farm Land with Unharvested Crops

Here is another tax break for farmers. Profit from unharvested crops is capital gains income if the underlying land is sold.

Drawbacks—This is another case of having to sell the goose in order to get the golden egg. You have to part with your farmland in order to obtain the capital gains treatment. Furthermore, recent changes in the Tax Law eliminate capital gains treatment if too much of it is received.

5. Orchards

This is similar to sale of farmland with unharvested crops. The costs of developing and maintaining an orchard are deductible. Later on, though, the orchard can be sold at capital gains rates.

Drawbacks—You'd damn well better know what you are doing if you get involved in the orchard business. Farming is tricky and speculative. You can lose your shirt at it, particularly if you try to do it on a small scale or on a part-time basis.

The first three years' costs of developing an orchard must be capitalized rather than deducted. If the orchard is sold prior to being held ten years, part of the gain may be ordinary income.

6. Capital Gains on Timber

Lumber companies get a tax break from the fact that part of the profit on timber they harvest is reported at capital gains rates. The capital gains portion is based on the tree's market value on the first day of the year in which it was cut. This tax break was put into effect years ago as an incentive for big lumber companies to conserve and reforest their timber lands.

Drawbacks—Unless you are a lumber company, it's pretty hard to take advantage of this one.

7. Gifts to Family Members

Normally, your children's tax brackets will be lower than your own. If you give them income producing assets—such as stocks, bonds, or rental properties—they will pay less tax on the income than you will.

Drawbacks—The gifts must be bona fide. That is, you have to permanently part with the assets. Furthermore, the gift's income cannot be used to pay for any of your children's support. Whatever support you are legally obligated for must still be paid from personal funds. Unless you are very wealthy, you probably need every bit of income you can get your hands on. Consequently, it wouldn't be practical to give any of it away even if you would save taxes. In addition, if you give over $3,000 in value away it may be subject to a gift tax.

8. Ten-Year Trusts

This is a way of saving taxes by making Indian gifts. By using a ten-year trust you don't permanently part with the assets. The gimmick is that you put income producing assets into a trust that lasts only ten years. Your kids receive the trust's income but at the end of ten years, the original assets go back to you.

Drawbacks—Again, you have to part with the use of the assets and their income for a minimum of ten years; none of the trust's income can be used to pay for your children's support; and you may have to pay a gift tax.

9. Getting Married

If you are now single, getting married, theoretically, will save you taxes. Filing a joint return causes your income to be averaged with that of your spouse, thereby subjecting it to lower tax brackets.

Drawbacks—A wife will cost you a lot more than any tax saved, I'll guarantee you that. Besides, getting married saves taxes *only* if your bride-to-be is *not* working. Due to some goofy quirks in the 1969 Tax Reform Act, a working couple pays less tax *not* being married than they do being married. For example, a man making $15,000 and a woman making $10,000 pay combined taxes of $4,523. If they marry, their taxes jump to $4,908, an increase of $385. Hallelujah! Shack up and save taxes. The I.R.S. has created a new reason for living in sin.

10. Deferred Salary Contracts

Highly paid executives and professional athletes sometimes have part of their salaries deferred until later years when, presumably, they will be in lower tax brackets.

Drawbacks—This isn't an advantage unless you are currently in high tax brackets. You are deprived of the use of the deferred salary until later years. It's possible that you could earn more on it currently even after taxes than the taxes you stand to save by deferring it. By the time you finally get it, inflation will likely have robbed you of part of your tax savings. Finally, your employer gets no salary deductions until he actually pays you off.

Conclusion

Originally, I had hoped to keep this chapter simple. I tried. Lord knows I tried. But dammit, it just isn't possible!

I hope you can now see that this business of tax shelters is complicated. Most so-called shelters are an advantage only in special situations or for a special category of people. The foregoing descriptions are generalizations of rules and regulations that are voluminous, intricate, constantly changing, and riddled with exceptions. Before implementing any of them, by all means seek advice from a professional tax advisor.

26

Sidestepping Tax Traps

There is one difference between a tax collector and a
taxidermist—the taxidermist leaves the hide.

Mortimer Caplan,
Former Commissioner of Internal Revenue

Tax planning isn't so much a matter of finding loopholes.
Mainly it's learning how to sidestep tax traps. Loopholes are
pretty much a thing of the past. By now most of them have been
plugged. Lawyers, intoxicated by the smell of fat fees, have over
the years sought out loopholes like pigs rooting up truffles. Many
have been found. The trouble is, the I.R.S. always comes along
later and covers them back up.

The pattern is always the same. Some ingenious tax advisor
discovers an overlooked quirk in the law that is favorable to
taxpayers under the right set of circumstances. He maneuvers his
clients so as to be able to take advantage of it. They, in turn, brag
to their friends at the country club about the gimmick. The word
gets around. Soon the tax advisor is being referred additional
clients. Other tax advisors seek his advice. He is called upon to give
speeches on the subject at professional meetings. The tax advisory
services publicize the technique in their periodic tax bulletins.
Professional trade journals publish it for their members.

Soon the I.R.S. becomes concerned. They challenge the
original loophole exploiters in the tax court. The I.R.S. loses. The

loophole is now sanctioned by the courts. Everybody and his brother starts using it. The I.R.S. muckymucks become alarmed. They feel that utilization of the tax laws in this manner violates the original intent of Congress. So the I.R.S. goes back to Congress and asks that the laws be amended to close the loophole. It may take a few years, but eventually Congress complies.

This whole process from beginning to end takes time, but it always runs its course. The point is that by now every conceivable loophole that could have been discovered has been plugged up, at least partially. America's brightest tax lawyers have gone over the Internal Revenue Code with microscopic probes. I.R.S. agents have followed, anti-leak sealant in hand. As soon as a loophole is discovered, they work like mad to stop it back up.

Tax traps, on the other hand, have not been subjected to this same process. The I.R.S., of course, works for the government. It is interested in exploiting tax traps—not eliminating them. Justice for the taxpayer is of no concern. The I.R.S.'s attitude is if Congress intended justice, then they should have legislated it. In the meantime, the I.R.S. doesn't care what they find in a tax trap—they'll skin it regardless.

Tax trap victims, unfortunately, are not well organized. They tend to be people of modest means who can't afford adequate tax counsel. Following are a few examples of the sort of things that can happen.

Example #1

Daddy Bigbucks, the millionaire, decides to start a new business—the manufacture of ganip-ganops. So his lawyers set up a new corporation and he puts $20,000 into it.

PeeWee McDew, the hard-working, middle-class slave, decides to go into the ganip-ganop business also. He too sets up a corporation and he contributes his hard-earned $20,000 of life's savings into it.

The ganip-ganop market suddenly goes to hell. Both Bigbucks and McDew lose their $20,000.

Comes the time to make out their annual income tax returns, Daddy Bigbucks deducts his $20,000 loss. Being in the 70% tax bracket, he recovers $14,000 in taxes, making his real ganip-ganop loss only $6,000. PeeWee McDew goes to a tax service to have his return prepared. He tells them about the $20,000 ganip-ganop corporation loss that he has suffered. The preparer says, "I am sorry, Mr. McDew, but losses from worthless stocks are capital losses. You can only deduct *one-half* of that loss at the rate of $1,000 a year." PeeWee McDew is incredulous, "But I lost $20,000! You mean all I can deduct is $1,000 of it this year?" "I'm sorry, Mr. McDew," says the tax advisor, "but that is the rule according to the tax laws."

Why was Daddy Bigbucks able to deduct the full $20,000 and all in one year? Because he could afford well-qualifed tax advisors, that's why. When he incorporated, they inserted a few simple little sentences in his corporation's bylaws. The sentences said that his corporation's capital stock was something called "Section 1244 Stock." These magic words are what entitled Daddy Bigbucks to favorable tax treatment.

The result: Daddy Bigbucks only lost $6,000 after his tax rebate. PeeWee McDew, being in the 25% bracket and only being able to deduct one-half, lost $17,500. Taking into consideration the present value of his tax rebate being spread out over ten years, he really lost about $18,500.

The ironic thing is that Section 1244 was originally enacted as a tax relief measure for small business. Yet, I have never encountered a small businessman who has actually benefited from it. The only people aware of Section 1244 are those, who, like Daddy Bigbucks, are affluent enough to be able to retain good tax counsel.

Example #2

Now, let's assume the opposite. Let's assume that the ganip-ganop businesses became thriving successes. After a few years both Daddy Bigbucks and PeeWee McDew decide to sell out.

Here is how Daddy Bigbucks sells out: Bigbucks' financial advisors interest the Ford Motor Company into buying his ganip-ganop corporation, which by now is worth $120,000. So, Ford Motor Company gives Daddy Bigbucks $120,000 worth of Ford Motor Company stock in exchange for his ganip-ganop stock. Bigbucks' stock, remember, originally cost $20,000, so he has a

$100,000 gain. What is his income tax on the transaction? Zero! The exchange of capital stock and control of a corporation solely for another corporation's stock is a tax-free exchange. (Section 368(a)(1)(B).)

Daddy Bigbucks has converted his original $20,000 investment into a secure, dividends paying, appreciating-in-value investment currently worth $120,000—tax free!

Now, watch what happens to good old PeeWee McDew. McDew also finds someone who is willing to pay $120,000 for his ganip-ganop company. Only his buyer can't pay cash so McDew offers him terms—30% down and the $84,000 balance payable over ten years. The buyer already has his own corporation. So, McDew simply has his ganip-ganop corporation sell all of its assets and liabilities to the buyer. Then McDew dissolves his corporation, distributing to himself the $36,000 down payment money and the $84,000 ten-year contract.

Here are the tax consequences to McDew:

Tax Trap #1

McDew's corporation must pay tax on the sale. McDew didn't sell his corporation; instead, he had his corporation sell its assets directly to the buyer. This constituted a separate transaction between the corporation and the buyer. Therefore, the corporation had a gain on which it must pay tax.

Tax Trap #2

Part of the corporation's gain is ordinary income. Normally, the sale of a business is capital gains income, only half of which is taxed. However, part of the assets sold by McDew's corporation consisted of equipment. When equipment is sold, the owner must take back as ordinary income the previous depreciation claimed as tax write-offs. This is known as the Section 1245 "depreciation recapture" rule.

Tax Trap #3

Even though the $120,000 sales price is spread out over ten years, the corporation must pay the entire tax on its gain all in one year. Normally, gains on installment sales can be reported as you receive the installment payments. However, when McDew liquidated his corporation and transferred the $84,000 sales contract to himself, he converted it into something known as a "disposition of an installment obligation." A disposition of an installment obligation causes its entire gain to become immediately taxed.

Tax Trap #4

McDew as an individual must also pay tax because he took the sales proceeds out of his corporation. His gain is measured by the difference between the net assets he received and the original cost of his ganip-ganop corporation's stock.

Final result: The corporation must pay a tax of $32,000 and McDew must pay a tax of $10,000. Total tax—$42,000. Total cash received from the down payment—$36,000. It cost McDew $6,000 out-of-pocket to sell his corporation!

Example #3

Daddy Bigbucks' deadbeat son-in-law hits him up for a $10,000 business loan. After consulting with his tax advisors (which he always does), Bigbucks says, "No, I won't loan you $10,000, but tell you what I will do: You go to the bank and borrow $10,000 using my signature as guarantor." The bank is only too happy to loan deadbeat son-in-law $10,000 since Bigbucks' signature is golden.

Son-in-law defaults on the loan, so Bigbucks has to pay the bank off as guarantor. At income tax preparation time, Daddy Bigbucks deducts the $10,000 as a loss. Since he is in the 70% bracket, he is really out only $3,000 after taxes.

PeeWee McDew's son-in-law hits him up for a $10,000 business loan also. PeeWee doesn't have $10,000 in cash lying around, but his credit is good so he goes to the bank and borrows it. Then he loans the $10,000 to his son-in-law and has him sign a promissory note. McDew's son-in-law goes bust and can't repay the $10,000.

Does McDew get a $10,000 loss deduction like Daddy Bigbucks did? No! His loss is a capital loss, which is deductible at the rate of only $1,000 per year. After tax rebates, he is out about $7,000 while Bigbucks lost only $3,000.

How come? Because Bigbucks didn't directly loan his son-in-law $10,000 like McDew did. He only guaranteed his son-in-law's loan at the bank. Section 166(5) allows complete write-offs of bad debts created from guaranteeing another individual's business loan. Losses from direct loans under exactly the same circumstances are short-term capital losses subject to limitations on their deductibility. Tough luck, PeeWee—ignorance of the law is no excuse, you know.

Example #4

Daddy Bigbucks owns 95% of the stock in a successful corporation. His son owns the other 5%. Bigbucks decides to get out and turn the corporation over to his son. So, he sells his stock back to the corporation at a substantial gain to himself. Since the only remaining outstanding stock is in the hands of his son, son winds up owning 100% of the corporation. Tax consequences to Bigbucks? His profit is long-term capital gains, only half of which is taxable.

PeeWee McDew does the very same thing with the 95% interest he has in his corporation. He retires, selling his stock back to the corporation, leaving his son in full control. PeeWee McDew should also get long-term capital gains, right? Wrong! McDew reports it that way, all right, but later his tax return is audited and the I.R.S. agent finds that McDew forgot to say the magic words again. Because his sale left a close relative (his son) in control of the corporation, McDew was supposed to include a special statement with his tax return. McDew was supposed to say words to the effect that, having sold his stock, he had no further interest in the corporation and that he agreed to inform the I.R.S. if he ever did reacquire an interest in the corporation at any time within the next ten years. Since such a statement was not filed, McDew lost out on capital gains treatment.

Example #5

Bigbucks decides to buy another business. He pays $70,000 for it. In addition, he pays the former owner $30,000 for a covenant not to compete. That is, in consideration for $30,000 the former owner agrees not to go into business again as a competitor for five years. Tax consequences—Bigbucks gets to deduct the $30,000 against ordinary income over the five year life of the noncompetition covenant.

Now, PeeWee McDew comes along and does the same thing—that is, *almost* the same thing. The difference is that McDew writes it up this way: He agrees to pay $100,000 for the business, same as Bigbucks. He also, being very cagey, has the former owner, as part of the purchase price, agree to a covenant not to compete. The only difference is that he makes the noncompetition covenant part of the purchase contract without specifying exactly how much of the total purchase price applies to it. What difference does that make? McDew is still going to pay $100,000 regardless of whether $1 or $99,000 is allocated to the covenant. Right, except that the I.R.S. allows you to deduct costs of a non-competition covenant only if the amount paid for it is specifically and separately set out.

Since PeeWee McDew didn't do that, he isn't allowed to deduct it. The I.R.S. makes him show the $30,000 cost of the noncompetition agreement as nondeductible good will.

———————————————————————

I bet it's been quite awhile since you last read *Alice in Wonderland,* hasn't it?

I could go on, but this should be enough to give you the idea. These sorts of things happen to people all of the time. How you are treated isn't so much a matter of *what* you do, but rather, *how* you do it. Often, magic words must be said. Often, special labyrinthic routes and elections must be followed. Unfortunately there is no way the average layman can learn these secrets. Even if he had the time to study the tax laws, he couldn't understand them. They are too complicated, too technical, too voluminous, and too subject to change.

So, if you go into business, seek out a good tax attorney or a good tax accountant, or both. The good ones command high hourly fees. This scares many small businessmen away. Actually, from a practical standpoint, tax advice isn't all that expensive —90% of the things you are liable to become involved with, a good tax specialist can answer right off the top of his head. The other 10% are probably well worth the cost of whatever time it takes to have him research the matter.

Finally, seek tax advice *before* the deal. If you wait until afterwards, it is usually too late to re-ring the bell.

27

Professional Advisors

Once there was a lawyer who was drifting on the ocean in a life raft with several other shipwreck survivors. Presently, the raft came close to a nearby island but since the waters were heavily populated by sharks, no one felt like jumping overboard to push the raft ashore. Finally the lawyer stood up and said, "I am not afraid." He leaped over the side and started swimming towards the island, pushing the raft before him as he went. A huge shark swam up to the raft. Instead of attacking the lawyer, it proceeded to swim beside him and help push the raft ashore. The raft's other occupants were incredulous. "Why," they asked the lawyer, "did that man-eating shark help you push the raft ashore?" "Just a matter of professional courtesy," replied the lawyer.

Anonymous Story Told by
an Anonymous Non-Lawyer

Maxim: Never trust a lawyer or a C.P.A. over 50 years old.

Corollary: Never trust a lawyer or a C.P.A. under 35 years old.

Believe it or not, law and accounting are intellectually demanding. There is much to know and learn these days.

Academic training isn't enough. Until someone has had at least ten years of practical experience in the field, he just isn't worth much. So, don't hire a professional advisor unless he is at least 35. By that age he will have made a lot of mistakes—at his clients' expense. By coming along later on in his career, you will benefit from the hard-earned experience that others have paid for.

The intense demands of the legal and accounting professions cause early flame-outs. By age 50, a lawyer or a C.P.A. will have been through a lot and won't feel like going through much more. Twenty-five years of long hours, tensions, frustrations, unreasonable clients, and modest pay will have taken their toll. By 50, a lawyer or a C.P.A. will usually have brought junior associates into the firm to do his dirty work. Unless you're a large, important account, you'll never have the benefit of the older guy's experience. He'll have brief conferences with you now and then but it will be some peon in the back office actually doing your work. You are better off to hire "young" middle-aged professional advisors between the ages of 35 and 50 who still have some get up and go left in them.

Now, let me say this about professional fees: You may not always get what you pay for, but you for darn sure always have to pay for what you get. Any lawyer or C.P.A. who is any good won't work cheap. So don't shop around for bargains. If you pay cheap fees, you'll get cheap work. And cheap legal and accounting services always backfire. In the long run, faulty advice, or non-advice, will cost you a lot more than any fees you save.

Find out the professionals' fee arrangements in advance. That way there shouldn't be any surprises. It isn't possible for them to tell you ahead of time exactly how much their services will cost, but at least they should be able to give you a rough idea.

Generally speaking, it is harder to find a good C.P.A. than it is a good lawyer. This is because, as a person, a C.P.A. is more difficult to judge. C.P.A.'s, as a rule, tend to be cautious, conservative, intelligent, introvertish, and bland. If you were looking for an antonym to the word "charisma" you wouldn't be far wrong choosing "C.P.A." C.P.A.'s tend to be the kind of people you do not think of when making up a guest list for a party. Being sensitive souls by nature, they are only too painfully aware that their personalities have the blahs. Realizing that being an introvert has drawbacks in business, some C.P.A.'s try to overcome their natural predispositions by joining toastmaster clubs and assuming the external coloration of extroverts. In this pursuit they are no more successful than anyone else attempting a personality transformation. C.P.A.'s trying to be extroverts tend to adopt exaggerated hail-fellow-well-met affections, liberally sprinkled with nervous laughs and hysterical grins. But if you shake hands with one, you'll discover that his palms are sweaty.

In addition to personality problems, C.P.A.'s constantly have to fight a status gap. Nearly everybody puts them down when it comes to status. Doctors, lawyers and other professionals look down on the accounting world's lack of intellectual achievement. Peruse the literature of the American Institute of C.P.A.'s for example, and you'll be amazed at how so little substance can be contained in such a large volume of words. Upper-level business managers usually consider auditors to be pimples on the face of progress. White collar workers think of accountants as being low-down on the Corporation's status totem pole. Blue collar workers consider accountants to be pencil-pushing sissies, totally lacking in physiques robust enough to perform physical labor. And the lower classes think that C.P.A. probably stands for Cleaning, Pressing and Alterations.

These derogatory attitudes could be overcome if accountants made a lot of money. Possession of wealth automatically carries considerable status along with it. But most accountants drive Chevrolets rather than Cadillacs.

This unfortunate image makes it very difficult for C.P.A.'s to establish any kind of self-respecting rapport with clients. The business and social pressures put upon them combine with their uptight emotional make-ups to create high blood pressure, ulcers, and nervous tics.

I'm not being facetious about the tics. Many C.P.A.'s do have nervous mannerisms. I remember an older partner of a C.P.A. firm I once knew, who had the disconcerting habit of scratching his crotch whenever things got tense. This was always a source of considerable embarrassment to his younger partners, for the old boy would sometimes absentmindedly perform his habit in front of clients, irrespective of whether they were male or female. It wasn't just a furtive scratch either, but, rather, a mauling, clutching grab. One time three of this particular firm's partners were having a conference regarding the application for employment of a young college graduate. It happened to be a very busy time of year, so all three were exhibiting nervous tic symptoms. One, the gentleman just described, was busy scratching himself. The second was shuffling his feet on the floor, that being his particular specialty. The third was tugging at his collar and making faces. One of the three remarked that he didn't think that the young applicant should be hired because he appeared to be too nervous to stand up under the pressures of being a C.P.A.!

Lawyers and C.P.A.'s are no different than doctors. There is a wide range of competency between individuals. Just because someone has met the minimum standards necessary to enter his profession doesn't mean that he is capable of meeting your needs. Now, I grant you that it is hard for laymen to judge relative capabilities of professionals. Professionals deal in esoterics and they don't, as a rule, criticize each other. Doctors bury their mistakes but you have a better chance with lawyers and C.P.A.'s. Lawyers and C.P.A.'s may also try to conceal their goofs from you, but at least with them you stand a chance of catching them at it. If you're curious about the way they handled something or the way something they handled turned out, ask them to explain it to you. Chances are you won't be able to understand the finer points of the explanation given you, but if they use a lot of weasel words or grandiose generalities—watch out!

Once you've chosen a C.P.A. and a lawyer, the key is—use them for preventive medicine. See your lawyer and C.P.A. *before* you do something, not after . . . especially your lawyer. I see businessmen all the time who have gotten themselves into legal jackpots because they were too cheap to consult an attorney. The same thing applies to accountants. Guys come into my office all the time with tax problems they wouldn't have had if they'd seen me *before* they did the deal.

The real value of a lawyer is to help you *avoid* lawsuits. Lawsuits can be horrendously expensive. They can also be very trying on your nerves. I can't emphasize too much the importance of trying to avoid them. Despite the virtuousness of your case, you always stand a chance of losing once you get into the courtroom. Business disputes often result in capricious judgments because many times they involve issues that the judge, jury, and attorneys don't really understand.

Newcomers to business have a tendency to regard business disputes as affairs of honor. They feel that they will lose face if they don't go to court over an issue. Saving face in the business world is a time-consuming, costly luxury. Sometimes you cannot escape winding up in court over a particular matter, but you should try to conduct your affairs in such a manner so as to make this a rare occurrence. Consult your attorney ahead of time and often. A few minutes of conversation with him can often save you many future hours of grief and frustration.

As long as we are discussing professional advisors, I suppose something should be said about business consultants. What will be said is this—consultants at the small business level are a fraud and a waste of money. I have had a number of clients hire so-called consultants and their experience has been uniformly bad.

Consulting a consultant has great appeal when a whole lot of problems are nipping at your heels. Consultants do, after all, hold themselves out as being professional problem solvers. What they actually are is professional magic wand wavers. What they are selling is confidence. What they say, in essence, is, "I am the Great Wizard. I am an expert and an infallible brain. Hire me and I will show you the light; I will solve your pressing problems."

As a practical matter, when he gets all through with it, a consultant's report usually winds up as a jargon-ated enumeration of all of his clients' problems, which, as it turns out, the client was already well aware of.

In the late 1940's, before management consulting became the high priest type activity it presently is, a prominent management consultant explained his practice as being mainly the application of common sense. This honest insight still holds true today, especially where small business consulting is concerned. So don't be conned into thinking that a business consultant has any special magic to offer. If a consultant is really any good he won't be fooling around with small business engagements to begin with because the potential fees are too small.

As to your attorney, here are some things you'd better have him do for you:

1. Help you decide the form of doing business.
2. Draft a written partnership agreement.
3. Draft a buy-sell agreement with your partners.

4. Review *all* contracts and agreements *before* you sign them.

5. Review the details of all long-term financing arrangements.

6. Review the legal ramifications of any new ventures you are thinking of undertaking.

Here are some things you should have your C.P.A. do for you:

1. Set up your accounting system.

2. Set up a system of internal control for your assets.

3. Help you with loan application presentations.

4. Represent you before the Internal Revenue Service. (Don't talk to the I.R.S. yourself. I.R.S. agents are real skilled at getting you to put your foot in your mouth.)

5. Periodically review your books and analyze your financial statements.

6. Help you prepare budgets and projections.

Finally, make sure your attorney and your C.P.A. earn their fee, but don't begrudge it to them. Very few attorneys and C.P.A.'s servicing small business clientele die wealthy, believe me.

28

How to Make People Pay You the Money They Owe

Something that initiates people very quickly to the facts of business life is the discovery that it is damn hard sometimes to collect on your accounts receivable. When half of your receivables are delinquent or slow, it puts a real crimp in cash flow. Especially if your profit margin is only 5 or 10 percent.

Now, normally, the reason people don't pay their bills isn't because they don't have the money. Rather, it is because they don't have enough money to pay all of their bills *at the same time.* Accordingly, they follow the squeaky wheel principle. They pay whomever yells at them the loudest. People who don't yell get put down at the bottom of their payment list.

The secret, then, in collecting money is to yell loud and long and often. "When are you going to pay your bill? . . . I thought you said you were going to mail me a check last week? . . . I need payment immediately, if not sooner! . . . Pay up, now!"

The trouble is, most people really don't like to do this sort of thing. Collecting is a distasteful activity. Nevertheless, it is necessary. Not putting the squeeze on delinquent debtors dooms you to sharing their same fate. Soon, you too won't have enough money to pay all your bills at the end of the month.

It is best to accompany your yelling with threats. Threaten to put your debtors on C.O.D. (Cash on Delivery); or to not sell to them anymore unless they bring their accounts current; or to turn them over to a collection agency. Of course, nobody likes to alienate customers. You may be reluctant to get too hard–nosed with a large customer for fear of losing his future business. If so, the next best thing to threats is to hit him with polite requests that are frequent. Squeak softly, but often. Adopt the technique many wives use: Nag, Nag, Nag!

The point is, don't depend on a delinquent debtor's conscience. Unless you bug him, you'll invariably wind up sitting at the bottom of his bill pile.

So much for slow receivables. Then there is the other kind. The kind that are not only slow but potentially bad debts as well. The best approach towards reducing bad debts is to not create them in the first place.

Credit policy is similar to the life insurance business. It is a game of statistics. If you take chances, you are going to take losses. Institute liberal credit, personal check cashing, and soft collection policies and you will have bad debts—the statistics demand it. Inexperienced businessmen usually start out being much too liberal when it comes to credit because they are afraid of losing hard-to-come-by sales. What they don't realize is that, if they lose a sale, all they are losing is the profit. On the other hand, if they lose a bad debt, they not only lose the profit, they also lose the cost of the merchandise as well. I am a strong believer in tough credit policies and I was originally going to advise that you be very careful to whom you extend credit. However, nobody ever pays any attention to this sort of advice, so I'm not going to bother giving it. I know from personal experience that when you're scraping and scratching for business and some questionable customer dangles a dollar in front of you, nine times out of ten you'll make a grab for it. Anxiety for new business overcomes most small operators' doubts as to the credit of potential customers. So they don't bother asking for credit references or having their banks run credit checks or asking for advance deposits and cash on delivery. Instead they wait until a debt goes sour before coming to their senses.

For this reason, I am going to resist the temptation of saying that most bad debt problems can be avoided by being discriminating at the time of sale. Instead, I am going to concentrate on how to collect doubtful receivables once they've already been created.

Fast action is the important thing. Chances are the guy owes a lot of other people besides yourself so it's a matter of who gets to him first. If you wait too long to act, you'll wind up being left out every time.

Being small, you can't afford a collection department so you'll either have to turn him over to an outside collection agency or an attorney. Collection agency fees range somewhere between 25% to 50% of whatever is collected, depending upon the size of the debt. Attorneys usually charge roughly the same except that they may want to be paid on an hourly basis if the debt is really of doubtful collectibility.

I think collection agencies are a little more efficient than most attorneys because usually they've had more experience at it. Of course, if the debt is large and you know you'll probably have to sue for it, you might as well turn it over to your attorney early because he'll have to become involved sooner or later anyway.

One of the quickest ways to collect is to simply have your attorney garnish, or attach, the debtor's bank account. This always gets a fast response. The trouble is, you have to know where the debtor's bank account is located. Also, you can be countersued for damages by the debtor if he can prove it was a wrongful attachment. The trend of recent judicial decisions has been to restrict garnishments to situations where there has been due process of law. It is also possible to garnish a debtor's salary if he is employed. Here again, the judicial trend has been to at least require a hearing before allowing the garnishment. In addition, most states allow a certain portion of the debtor's salary to be exempt even if the garnishment is valid. At any rate, this is a procedure that you will have to leave up to your attorney.

If you do have to take a guy to court, winning a judgment still might not get you your money. All a judgment means is that the court agrees with you that it is a legitimate debt. However, the debtor may still refuse to pay up. If so, your only recourse is to find some asset of his that your local sheriff can go out and levy upon. But you yourself will have to find his attachable assets. The sheriff won't go running around the country for you looking for something of the debtor's to grab. Still, there are advantages to getting a judgment. For example, once a judgment has been recorded in the local recorder's office, it becomes a lien against any real estate the debtor may own.

As you can see, collecting is a problem because it costs you both time and money. The trouble is, all dyed in the wool deadbeats know this too. Some of them may use this knowledge against you in an attempt to compromise their debts. An experienced deadbeat may say, "O.K., tell you what: I'll pay you off if you cut my bill in half. Otherwise, you'll have to sue me for it." This is a sneaky, but effective, ploy. The debtor knows that you know that what with attorney's fees and all, one-half is all you'll get anyway if you sue him. Besides, suing takes time. So many people faced with a situation like this do wind up compromising. I think it's best to call the deadbeat's bluff (assuming that there is no *legitimate* argument over the bill). Being sued costs him money too so if you stick to your guns, he'll probably become anxious to settle somewhere short of actually going to court.

Another trick of deadbeats is to send you a partial payment with something like, "Acceptance of this check constitutes payment in full," typed on the face of the check. I've had conflicting opinions from attorneys as to the validity of such statements. To avoid hassles it's probably best for you to simply return the check.

I have been told that one way to cut down on collection expense is to have wording printed on your invoices to the effect that, by accepting the merchandise, the customer agrees to assume all subsequent costs of collection including attorneys' fees. I've never actually had any of my clients do this but it sure sounds like a good idea. If it is written in small print, it probably won't bother anybody. Another manuever on your part is to have delinquent customers sign promissory notes. Promissory note forms usually bear interest and call for all future collection costs to be borne by the debtor. In addition, once a note is signed, it automatically fixes the amount owing. This makes it easier for you to sue the debtor later on if he defaults. For this reason, experienced deadbeats are usually reluctant to sign promissory notes.

If you are a subcontractor, it's possible for you to insure payment from the general contractor by filing what is known as a "materialman's lien." This is a lien that attaches to the property you are working on. The trouble is, materialman's liens usually have to be filed shortly after your work is completed (within 30 days in many states). Most subcontractors don't like to take such drastic action so soon—it might sour their relationship with the general contractor if it turns out afterwards that it wasn't actually necessary.

You can avoid collection expenses on small debts by suing the debtor yourself in a small claims court. It isn't necessary to be represented by an attorney in small claims courts. Proceedings are rather informal. The amount you can sue for, though, is usually limited to not more than a few hundred dollars. Also, small claims courts have crowded calendars so you may have to waste a lot of your own time waiting around for a hearing.

Collecting money is a disagreeable task. It's an expense and a bother that most neophyte businessmen don't count on when first contemplating going into business for themselves. Consequently, they aren't prepared for just how much of a hassle it usually turns out to be. Regardless of its unpleasantness, you can't ignore it. Benign neglect doesn't make collection problems go away—it just lets more of them in the door.

29

How Not to Pay People the Money You Owe

Sooner or later there comes that humiliating, panic stricken, ignominious day when you add up your bills and find that you are short. There isn't enough money to pay them all. You've already borrowed up to the hilt at the bank. Obviously, some creditors are going to have to wait. Whom don't you pay first?

Your strategy as a debtor must be just the opposite of what it was when you were a creditor. Pay no attention to the noises various creditors make. Instead, sit down with your bills and try to classify them all as to their relative importance. The classification you come up with determines who gets paid first.

There are three rough categories into which all your bills can be sorted:

1. The *they-can-shut-off-your-water* type of bills;

2. The *they-can-make-it-uncomfortable-for-you* type of bills; and

3. The *they-can-wait* bills.

Category (1) bills are those that you are going to have to pay just to keep your doors open. Utilities are a prime example. The water, power and telephone companies can shut you off right now if you become delinquent. They will too, because utility companies don't mess around.

Also included in Category (1) are Federal payroll taxes withheld from employees. Ironically, payroll taxes are one of the first things cash short businessmen usually get behind on. It's easy to do because the businessman himself must collect and pay them over to the Government. When you are short of money, the temptation to use withheld payroll taxes is very strong. Actually, they are a bad item to defer. The I.R.S. collection department is a rough customer. They'll come out and padlock your doors if you don't pay promptly. They can even pierce your corporate veil and go after you personally for back payroll taxes. Furthermore, penalties are steep—from 5% to 100%, plus 6% interest.

Usually there are a few key major suppliers or services who come under the shut-your-water-off category. These are the ones upon whom you depend for an ongoing supply of items vital to your business—the ones furnishing key ingredients to whatever it is that you sell. Somehow or other, you will have to keep these and all other Category (1) bills current.

Category (2) creditors are those that can make it uncomfortable for you but can't immediately put you out of business. They may have to go to considerable trouble in order to force collection. Examples are one-shot suppliers, or suppliers of items that can be obtained from many different sources. If they cut you off, you can acquire the same goods somewhere else after, perhaps, only a small delay. Unsecured bank loans come under this category. The bank will scream like crazy when you go delinquent but normally they can be stalled a long time before actually pulling your plug. As a matter of fact, once you get into a bank, they may even loan you more money to keep you going for fear of losing what is already owed them.

Category (2) types can be kept at bay quite awhile by simply giving them small partial payments. This is an important technique. No creditor has to accept partial payments but most of them do anyway. What makes creditors most nervous is not hearing from you at all. Silence is what turns collection departments on. A partial payment, on the other hand, lets them know you are still alive and in town and trying to pay them off. Throwing them a few bones won't necessarily make them happy but probably should forestall formal collection procedures on their part.

The tricky thing about partial payments is that you should make them to all Category (2) bills regardless of whether or not you have been getting any heat from them. Many debtors make the mistake of paying off in full those Category (2)'s that squawk a lot while ignoring those who remain silent. Then, all of a sudden, one of the polite, silent creditors turns out to be a sleeper and swoops down with a vengeance and maybe even forces you into involuntary bankruptcy.

Category (3) bills are those that you can get by not paying on at all for a long period of time. Most small bills come under this category—like office supplies, dues and subscriptions, small repair bills, printing bills, charge cards, cleaning bills, etc. When a bill is small like, say, under $50, it can cost more to collect it than the bill itself is worth. Hence, small balance creditors tend to be long-suffering. Legal and accounting bills are notorious they-can-wait types. Attorneys and accountants can't repossess anything and normally they are reluctant to sue debtor clients. Furthermore, if they refuse to continue servicing your account, you can probably always find other suckers to take their place.

Property taxes are commonly Category (3). In my home state, you can become five years delinquent before the property tax assessor forecloses. Furthermore, there is no personal liability as the property taxes are only a lien against the underlying property.

Nonpayment of bills strategy is a matter of deciding which category everything falls into. Take mortgage payments, for instance. Often you can stall a long time before having to catch back up on delinquent mortgage payments. Mortgage companies usually react slowly to delinquencies. They are reluctant to start formal foreclosure proceedings because of not really wanting the underlying mortgaged property back on their hands, although their attitude on this has been changing recently because of the high interest rates now in existence. If the mortgage has a low interest rate in terms of current rates, they may be quite willing to foreclose.

Sometimes landlords will tolerate several months of late rent payments before getting hard–nosed. Eviciting you from the premises may be expensive for them. Besides, you'll usually have one or two months' extra rent on deposit with them anyway as one of the original requirements of your lease.

One way of getting unsecured creditors to go along with you is to hint that they are in danger of forcing you into bankruptcy. That, generally, is the last thing they want to have happen. Experienced unsecured creditors know that, by the time attorneys, accountants, administrators and preferred and secured creditors get through picking your bankrupt bones, nothing much will be left over for them. Their chances are usually much better letting you continue operating. As a matter of fact, major creditors will sometimes even defer a customer's old balance and continue supplying him materials on a pay-as-you-go basis. The idea being that the current sales earn them current profits and, at the same time, make it possible for the debtor-customer to earn enough to eventually pay back the old balance.

You create settlement minded creditors for yourself any time you get them believing there is a reasonable chance your business may fail. The Minimax Principle of game theory takes a hold of them: Settling for fifty cents on the dollar may be the lowest maximum recovery they get, but, at the same time, it will be the highest minimum they can lose. They would rather, in other words, have a 100% chance of getting 50% of their money than take a 50% chance of getting 100% or 0%.

So don't hesitate to poor mouth yourself when talking to creditors. Most debtors do just the opposite. They give their creditors a rosy picture of how things are looking up and how they're making money again and how they should be able to pay them off shortly. A creditor's normal reaction to this is, "Well, if things are going so great, how come you aren't paying me anything? You must be paying somebody, how come it isn't me?" As a result, he presses all the harder for payment.

When trapped on the phone by creditors, most novice debtors try to mollify their tormentors with such inanities as—"Oh, haven't we paid you for that yet? I'll get after the bookkeeper to make up a check for you right away." Or, "Gee, I guess we must have lost your invoice. Can you send us a duplicate?" Or, "The person who ordered that is no longer with us, but I'll check into it right away." Or, "I could have sworn we'd already paid that. Well, we'll take care of it next month then."

Rank amateurism. Such statements don't even save face because their perpetrators know they aren't to be believed. What the pros do is shut off the phone. All phone calls are filtered through a secretary and only those not from creditors are answered. Talking to creditors before you are ready to talk to them is a waste of time. It merely adds to your emotional trauma. It's hard enough working one's way out of a short working capital position without being tormented by duns. Only talk to those creditors whom you hope to arrange some kind of a deal with and, then, only when you are composed and ready for them.

If a creditor does, by chance, get through to you, the quickest way to brush him off is to level with him. Tell him flat out that you don't have the money right now to pay him but that you intend to as soon as possible. You don't know exactly when that will be but you are doing the very best you can. If he gets persistent or nasty, tell him to go ahead and sue, if he wants, but he won't get paid any sooner. For good measure, you might add that, if he wants to try putting you through bankruptcy, he can do that too if he's willing to settle for 10¢ on the dollar. Then hang up on him.

Bankruptcy, by the way, may be the answer if things get too bad. When I was growing up, bankruptcy had a terrible stigma attached to it, like being raped or flunking out of school. Nowadays, though, it seems to have become rather commonplace. Most of the people I know who have gone through bankruptcy seem to bounce right back into business again. After awhile, their credit seems to be just as good as it ever was. Many creditors look upon a bankrupt individual as being a relatively "clean" credit risk. The act of bankruptcy reduces the chance of his having any old debts ahead of theirs. In addition, the "bankruptee" has to wait five more years before he can declare bankruptcy again. On the other hand, the stouthearted, honorable fellows who stubbornly refuse to give up until every single last creditor is paid off, seem to stay behind the eight-ball indefinitely. Ironically, even if the die-hard hangers-on do succeed in repaying all debts, their credit rating is no better than that of someone who went bankrupt. The fact that they toughed it out and paid everybody off doesn't alter the fact that their official credit record shows them as having been chronically delinquent and slow.

The idea of bankruptcy is to wipe a debtor's slate clean of a hopeless situation and to give him the chance for a fresh start. If your corporation goes bankrupt, that doesn't mean that you as an individual also have to go bankrupt. As a stockholder, you are only responsible for those corporate debts you have personally signed for. If you do have to go through bankruptcy as an individual, you are permitted to exclude certain personal assets from the creditors. These vary from state to state, but generally you can keep a house, a car, your personal effects, the tools of your trade, and a small amount of cash. Some debts aren't extinguished by bankruptcy—for example, taxes, alimony payments and property obtained under false pretenses.

Most delinquent debtors react with mortification to their situation. They bumble and fumble and mumble. The thing to remember is—don't panic. Stay cool. Many businesses, even big ones, get into financial trouble now and then. So don't worry about losing face. It's just part of the business game. Like being tackled behind your own goal line for a safety.

Classify your debts in the order I have suggested. Then take care of them according to their priority. If things get hopeless, don't be afraid to think the unthinkable (bankruptcy). If you are able to work your way out of your financial mess, sit down and try to figure out what got you into trouble in the first place. Then make sure you don't make the same mistakes twice. If you're going to get yourself into financial trouble again, at least have enough class to think up some different way of doing it.

30

The Care and Feeding of Employees

The experienced business manager knows that his employees will include neurotics, self seekers, incompetents, and prima donnas. His success as a business manager is measured by his ability to take this unpromising amalgam and get the job done with the least amount of mayhem.

Anonymous

Be aware of your employees' egos. The biggest cause of employee dissatisfaction isn't low pay or poor working conditions. It's the feeling of insignificance. The feeling that what they are doing is piddling and unimportant. Insensate bosses foster such feelings by creating the impression that their employees aren't needed as individuals—that they are small cogs. Don't take either employees or their work for granted. Puff up their egos when their work warrants it—blast them when they fall down on the job, but don't just ignore them. Remember, a few judicious compliments can stimulate incentive as much as a raise.

_____

One of the most insidious traps a business owner can fall into is letting his employees get too close to him. Effective employer-employee relationships are impossible once employees become personal friends. The danger of this happening is especially acute in small firms. The fewer the number of employees, the closer their interaction with management. Stay aloof. If you don't, your status as boss will be shot. Some people are natural born leaders whose very presence commands respect. If you are one of those, congratulations. If not, then you'd better avoid chumminess with employees. Insist on a certain amount of formality. If your employees can't respect you as a person, at least they can respect your uniform.

───────────────────────────

The secret of good hiring is good firing. Competent, conscientious employees are hard to find. Most of the time, you'll have to try several people before finding the right one for the job. This means your having to go through a cycle of hiring and firing. Many small businessmen complete the hiring part of the cycle all right, but they choke up when it comes to the firing. It's an unpleasant thing having to fire someone, so many bosses avoid it except in cases involving gross provocation. Consequently, they wind up accumulating marginal employees and having to rationalize their weaknesses: "Well, Joe makes quite a few mistakes all right, and he's not too good handling customers sometimes, but he's been with us for five years now and he knows the business real well. It would probably take a long time to train somebody to replace him and, besides, he's an awfully nice guy."

This attitude is a mistake. Inefficient labor gets a small business into trouble faster than almost anything else. Labor is usually a company's biggest expense. Small operators just don't have the margin to be able to carry deadwood.

───────────────────────────

If you are squeamish about firing people, then it is just something you'll have to get over, that's all. When it becomes necessary, do it as quickly and cleanly as possible. The longer you wait, the harder it becomes. The job is easier if you can do it in such a manner so as not to mangle the firee's ego and pride. Complimenting the guy on a few things, even if you have to lie a little bit to do it, will help make the task more palatable. For example, if you have to ash-can an employee, point out to him that he has abilities that would be more useful in another line of work. This helps him salvage some face which, in turn, makes the job of firing him a little easier on you.

————————————————————

When hiring, always require applicants to submit written resumes that include their background, their previous job history, and their references. Always be sure to check with an applicant's previous employers. Take what they tell you with a grain of salt because previous employers very seldom really level with you. People usually don't like to bad mouth former employees when responding to formal inquiries. I even know of an instance where a known embezzler was highly recommended by the very employer she had embezzled from. It turned out that her previous employer wanted her to have the new job so she could earn enough money to pay back what she had stolen from him!

Despite the reticence of most references to be honest, you can still pick up some clues about an applicant by talking to them. You can usually find out whether or not a prospective employee is a real ding-a-ling if you talk to enough people.

————————————————————

Employment agencies can be useful in preliminarily screening applicants but don't depend on them too much. An employment agency's judgment is distorted by its eagerness for placement fees. They usually do very little actual checking into applicants' backgrounds.

————————————————————

Don't chew an employee out in front of your other employees, even if he has it coming. There is nothing more destructive to a person's ego than to lose face with his peers. A public dressing down will probably eliminate whatever chance you ever had of developing him into an effective future employee. In addition, berating someone in front of others makes you look like a Captain

Queeg type of petty tyrant. Instead, chew the culprit out in private.

_____

Employee Types to Avoid

• Applicants whose employment history includes many previous jobs of short duration. Invariably those people have some kind of personality problem.

• Applicants who are over-qualified for the position. There's too much of a chance they'll use you as a temporary stopover until something better comes along.

• Applicants who have been recently divorced. Insurance companies know that the chances of a person having an auto accident increase greatly right after divorce. The period of instability that causes this also causes poor work performance.

• Applicants who have little or no previous work experience. Training neophytes is too big an investment for you to be making. Leave that to the big companies.

• Applicants who are preoccupied with time consuming outside hobbies or activities. Generally speaking, an employee's private life is his own personal business. But people who have some kind of really big thing, or cause, in their lives just don't make stable employees.

• Applicants who are highly educated. Higher education, in some ways, is a curse. The more educated you become, the more you realize you don't know. Not only that, but the more you realize you can't ever know. These revelations lead to wishy-washiness. Higher education creates people who always understand the other person's point of view and people who are always unsure of their own position. Always remember—bigots make the best businessmen. They aren't so easily confused.

• Applicants who are relatives. Relatives usually turn out to be either bad employees, or very bad employees. And once you hire one, they become twice as hard to get rid of as a nonrelative. Establishing an effective employer-employee relationship is hard enough as it is without having the complication of the employee being your sister's only son besides.

• Applicants who are beautiful women. It's fun having a really gorgeous creature around to look at and that is exactly the problem. You and all of your male employees will be looking and drooling and fantasizing when you should be concentrating on your work.

Rarely do you find a beautiful woman who works hard. Beautiful women don't work hard because they don't have to. Male chauvinistic-pig employers are nearly always more permissive and tolerant towards beauties than uglies. Beautiful girls quickly learn that they need work at only about one-half the pace of their Plain Jane sisters in order to hold down the same job. This law of nature, however, can be used to your own advantage. I have one business acquaintance, for example, whose number one criterion for hiring females is that they be ugly. This guy's office help may not be much to look at but their efficiency is frightening.

———————————————————————————

I'm skeptical of fringe benefits. Fringe benefits are nice but money is nicer. It has been my experience that employees appreciate their compensation much more if it is in the form of cold, hard, cash. There is just no substitute for the incentive that the long green stuff provides.

———————————————————————————

There is one concept to being an employer that is late in coming for most people. That is this: the perfect employee doesn't exist. All employees have strengths and weaknesses. What you must do is find some way of utilizing their strengths while working around their weaknesses. For example, suppose you have some old dragon around who is one hell of a worker but who gets into a fight with whomever he or she comes in contact with. You are impressed by this person's ability but are sick and tired of all the squabbles and hassles that he or she precipitates. The solution is simple. Isolation. Stick the problem employee in a separate office and channel everything done through you. The point is, don't be adverse to working out individualized accommodations so as to take advantage of an employee's strong points. You have to be tolerant of a certain amount of idiosyncrasies. After all, you must have some too, or else you wouldn't be in business for yourself.

———————————————————————————

Don't try to buck the unions. Next to the Federal government itself, unions are probably this country's most powerful institution. They don't much go in for goon squad type tactics anymore, except in isolated instances, but their political and economic power is enormous. There is no such thing as negotiating with a major union. What the major unions want, they are eventually going to get.

There will be no change in this situation until the union pendulum swings too far—until union demands become so ridiculous that the general public itself becomes aroused. Until this happens, the most you can do is pass unproductive union raises on to the customer and to make sure that all your competitors are subject to the same rules.

As a small businessman, you are going to have to abide by union contracts. Trying to get around them is fruitless. I remember one client, for example, who was approached by several of his union employees for extra work. My client told them he couldn't let them work overtime because he couldn't afford the time and one-half rate that overtime hours required. "That's O.K.," said the employees, "go ahead and let us work overtime and we'll only charge you straight time. We need the extra money so straight time is all right with us."

My client agreed to this. Several years later, a couple of disgruntled employees that he had fired went to the union and informed on him. As a result, my client wound up having to go back and retroactively pay overtime premium based on their estimated overtime hours. This was so even though the informing employees were the very ones who instigated the original straight time agreement!

31

The Law of Least Bungles

I saw Holmes put his hand to his forehead like a
man distracted. He stamped his feet upon the ground.
"He has beaten us, Watson. We are too late."
"No, no, surely not!"
"Fool that I was . . ."

Sherlock Holmes,
"The Hound of the Baskervilles"
by Sir Arthur Conan Doyle

Every enlisted man knows that armies do not win wars
because of the brilliance of their commanders. Rather, one army
wins because it happens to commit less bungles than the other.

Every week, half of America's football coaches declare to the
press, "We beat ourselves with our own mistakes."

Every losing politician knows in his heart that he would be
ensconced in City Hall right now if it weren't for his campaign
manager's boo-boos.

There is a common thread running throughout here. The
success of man's enterprises is a function of the mistakes made
rather than the quality of the strategy employed. The same
principle of war, sports, and politics also holds true in business.

Hence, Frost's Law of Least Bungles: "The success of a business is inversely proportional to the weight of its accumulated bungles."*

Every individual bungle made has a certain amount of detrimental effect on a businessman's situation. The detrimental effects of many bungles accumulate like radioactive sludge. Small businesses are highly unstable affairs. When the weight of their accumulated bungles reaches their critical mass, they self-destruct.

Most small businessmen intuitively recognize this. Unfortunately, this leads them into a faulty decision making habit. Knowing intuitively that big, important decisions have large amounts of potential bungle mass associated with them, the average businessman puts off making big decisions fearing that if he bungles one of them, it will seriously hurt his business.

Most small businessmen, therefore, favor making a lot of small, unimportant decisions rather than a few big ones. They spend more time making sure secretaries don't waste paper clips than they do trying to eliminate waste in the production line. More time is spent selecting the company car than is spent analyzing the company's financial problems. More thought is put into the annual Xmas party than is put into improving the company's products.

What these people fail to realize is that not making a decision is a decision in itself. Ignoring an important decision is to leave it to chance. Unfortunately, the vagaries of chance are more likely to result in a major bungle than the activity of making the decision itself. With a little experience, the average businessman over age 40 can make the right decision approximately 58½% of the time. This

---

*Frost's Law of Least Bungles can be expressed quantifiably as follows:

$$\text{Bungle Value (B)} = \frac{1}{1 - \sum_{t1}^{t2} bm\left(\frac{1}{M}\right)}$$

$\sum_{t1}^{t2} bm$ is a mathematical expression representing the sum of the masses (detrimental effects) of all the bungles made in a business from time (t1) to time (t2). When this term reaches the business' critical mass (M), the formula reduces to: $B = \frac{1}{0} = \infty$ (infinity), an impossible situation so that that particular business ceases to exist!

might not seem like much of an improvement over the 50-50 laws of chance, but it will still probably be enough to give an advantage over most other operators. Bungling, after all, is relative. To be successful over one's competitors, one needs only to have a lower bungle-value than they have. At any rate, the amount of bungle mass you eliminate by spending your time on small problems will never exceed and will never compensate for the bungle mass created by turning your important decisions over to the laws of chance.

This brings up the subject of "rearorities." Most people have little difficulty establishing a list of priorities for themselves. The problem the average small businessman has, however, is that he just doesn't have enough time to take care of all of his problems regardless of how they are arranged. Even with a priority list, he is still going to have to ignore some problems altogether. Deciding which to ignore is a much harder decision then merely listing things in the order of their importance. Small problems can be, and often are, more unpleasant emotionally than large ones. It is far easier to sit on a mountain than it is to sit on a tack.

Most small businessmen, therefore, fall into the habit of using the "squeaky wheel" method of problem solving. They tend to pay attention to whatever problem is making the greatest noise at the moment.

A more logical way of operating is to establish a list of rearorities. Start your list with those problems that you are going to consciously and purposely let go to hell. The problems at the top of your list are the ones you are not going to bother yourself with. If you don't have enough time during the day for everything, consult your rearority list for the things you are not going to get done. Of course, to do this, you are going to have to gird yourself and steel your mind against all the squeaks and screams that these neglected little problems will make. This is not an easy thing to endure. Every once in awhile you will probably have to give in to one or two of them just for the sake of your own peace of mind. Otherwise, a steady barrage of neglected small problems turns into a form of Chinese water torture.

The reason, I'm sure, that so many people have trouble with this concept of problem solving is because Frost's Law of Least Bungles is a law of accretion, or slow, cumulative effect. One doesn't tend to notice one's accumulated bungles until a lot of bungle mass has already built up. The effect of the large, silent, ignored problems isn't noticed while you are concentrating on all the small, noisy problems.

With these few principles in mind, you can start attacking your problems in a more efficient manner. In the future, spend time on problems based on their potential bungle-value rather than their noisiness. Decrease your accumulated bungle mass by not leaving large problems to chance. Take advantage of the Law of Least Bungles.

32

Epilogue

Pity a man for he don't know,
    the trouble he'll pass goin'
    down life's road . . .
He worked hard all his life to
    get things the way he
    wants 'em.
He comes here against his will—
    and he goes away disappointed.*

                Singer Glen Campbell,
                "Fate of Man"

The older, the more educated, and the more experienced I become, the more irresistibly I am drawn to the conclusion that, with respect to the overall scheme of things and taking into account the unfathomable spacetime vastness of the Universe—our individual lives don't mean diddly squat. Consciously or subconsciously, most people with any reflection time on their hands must eventually come to feel this way. Either that or they evolve into some form of madness. There is no other way to rationalize the basic absurdity of our existence. Out of the billions of spermatozoa manufactured by our fathers and out of the hundreds of ova left lying in wait in our mothers' wombs, why was our own particular DNA combination allowed to come to fruition? What purposes do our daily wanderings have? If you examine the average person's life, it seems to have about as much significance

---

*Quoted from "Fate of Man" by Glen Campbell. Used with permission of Glen Campbell Music, Inc.

as the random walk of a drunk. Yet, historically, man has always certified his supposed uniqueness from the other creatures of the planet. Man's religious dogmas consider him to be just one step below God, an important object of creation, worthy of God's attention. The more information modern science unravels from the Universe, however, the less unique and the less important we as individuals actually seem to be.

"All science is simply a great massing of proof that God, if He exists, is really neither good nor bad, but simply indifferent—an infinite Force carrying on the operation of unintelligible processes without the slightest regard, either one way or the other, for the comfort, safety, and happiness of man." (H.L. Mencken.)

We who live today are essentially the same animals physically and spiritually as our ancestors of 100,000 years ago. In those days, we eked out a marginal existence in small tribes, hunting, scrounging, picking berries, and digging roots. Millions of years of natural selection molded our species' traits to be suited to this type of existence. Inadvertently, we have created a bewildering environment for ourselves in which our old instinctive responses are mostly inappropriate. Our drives for social dominance and status, our desire for territory, our impulse to physically hurt those whom we imagine do us wrong, our instinct to beget offspring and heirs, our inability to identify with large groups or abstract causes—these characteristics, in the context of today's environment, are a recipe for disaster.

Homo Sapiens—nature's ultimate paradox. Insanely cruel and murderous on the one hand, angelically benevolent and kind on the other. The race that produces Bach and Beethoven likewise produces Hitler and Buchenwald. Surely by now philosophers must concede that man's conflicting nature cannot be centrifuged apart. It is apparent that Homo Sapiens is obsolete. In addition to basic structural similarities, there is one other characteristic we share in common with all other animals: Man is not an end in himself—he is just one more transition in the flowing stream of evolution.

Nietzsche's words come home to roost: "Man is merely a transition—a bridge over a chasm—an intermediate step between beast and superman." No amount of intellectual insight, no amount of eloquent moral persuasion can change man's basic nature. He must somehow evolve into something he isn't.

Either he must destroy his temples and his toys and go back to the Stone Age, or—

He must resign himself to playing the role of a dressed-up circus ape, cavorting in an artificial environment, or—

He must reshuffle his genes.

Only the latter option makes sense. The time is at hand when man should create a new species of super-intellects to take his place. When this inevitable event occurs, what the more realistic intellectuals have long suspected will be a demonstrable fact. All individual men's lives become as significant as so many ants on a sidewalk. If you want current proof, fly over Greater Los Angeles County, or spend a night on a mountain top, contemplating the stars.

In the meantime, out of respect for our ancestors and in response to our instincts, we, the now living, must somehow avoid madness as we twaddle away time waiting for our individual deaths to arrive. Man's emotions and glands are unimpressed by his intellects' assessment of futility and alienation. As hedonists, we don't ask questions, we seek fun. To this end, we need games to occupy ourselves with while we wait. We need purposeful activities to divert our minds. In the world's underdeveloped countries, the hassle of just trying to stay alive until old age fills the bill. Trying to satisfy the instinct for survival occupies all of one's time in Bangladesh. People in affluent countries, however, have time on their hands. It increasingly becomes a problem—how do we occupy ourselves to keep from going nuts? What will we do with three-day weekends?

Drugs, alcohol, meditation, sex (perverted and otherwise), politics, social climbing, mysticism, the arts, individual fame, religion, sports—whatever the salvation, all end up being trips in revolving squirrel cages.

But this much I can assure you: If you busy yourself with the problems of economic survival in a small business enterprise, if you depend upon a small business to feed, clothe, and support your family, you will not be bored. When you enter the small business jungle, you are reentering the arena of the old-fashioned fight for survival. What I mean to say is—you will have to hustle, you will have to frantically scramble.

But there are rewards. Besides its capacity to cause us to occupy our time, small business teaches a great deal about life in general. The relationships small business brings about expose many insights into human nature. Being in a constant state of competition with employees, customers and business rivals, you will quickly find out, if you don't know so already, that competing with a man for money is like getting him drunk—both tend to bring out his true character.

If you have the opportunity of dealing with the public long enough, you may even come to discover one of life's most startling secrets: Man's irrationality is the only thing that keeps him from going crazy, and often, the key to personal happiness is his ability to deceive himself.

Then, too, a small business career pumps up your self esteem. Whether you are successful or not, while you are at it, you will be the sole source of your own support. However minimal the importance your enterprise may have to the outside world, it will always give you a sense of accomplishment from the sheer fact that it provides you your daily sustenance. This is basic satisfaction—like the primeval joy of bringing down the stag.

Most of all, however, owning your own business guarantees that you will experience a full, lifetime range of emotions and feelings. There is nothing quite like, for example:

The cold sweat that breaks out over your body as the process server stands before you with a document indicating that someone is going to sue you for everything you've got . . .

Or, the depth of the sinking feeling you have when you've got a payroll to meet Friday and an overdraft plus an overdue note at the bank . . .

Or, the humiliating ignominy of having a credit collector call and tell you to cut out the flaky excuses . . . pay up now, immediately, or else . . .

Or, the empty panic that creeps over your soul when your backlog of orders shrivels up to nothing and you've got five more years' payments to make on your equipment . . .

Or, the castoff, rejected, loneliness you feel when you find out that your best customer has taken his business elsewhere . . .

Or, the glow of satisfaction that occurs when you add up the figures and discover that you've exceeded last year's profit . . .

Or, the thrill of having a customer compliment you on the job you've done . . .

Or, the little bump your ego gets every time you see your name on the door . . .

Or, the pride you feel when your son enters the business . . .

Or, the blessedness of the relief that sweeps over you as you make the final payment to the bank . . .

Or, the delicious, evil power you secretly feel after you've fired someone . . .

Or, the most ultimate satisfaction of all that comes when you realize you can make it on your own—you can stand on your own two feet.

There you have it, I have tried to outline how someone interested in running a small business can survive. I have tried to show that, essentially, it is a tough proposition and that small business is becoming an endangered species in today's economic structure. I have tried to point out that, nevertheless, it deserves preservation and that more people should try it. We must, after all, cling to those formats in our culture that are compatible with our basic nature.

The present situation is grim for small business but do not expect it to continue that way. The opportunity that small business affords is one part of the American Dream that is sacred. Once common, everyday Americans come to realize what small business is up against, the next popular political issue will have been born. Surely steps will be taken to reverse the trend.

So, go ye now forth, little small businessman, and be of good cheer. Good luck, God bless you, devil miss you, and may your epitaph read, "He tried his damndest!"

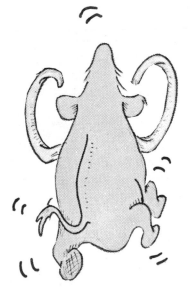